Istanbul
& the Aegean Coast

Front cover: the signature sight of
Ottoman Istanbul – domes piled on
domes as far as the eye can see
Below: the Süleymaniye Mosque

TOP 10 ATTRACTIONS

Bosphorus by ferry A trip along the famous strait, with lots to see on the way *(page 63)*

St Saviour in Chora •
One of the world's greatest monuments to Byzantine art *(page 49)*

The Süleymaniye The 16th-century Mosque of Süleyman the Magnificent is the finest Ottoman building in Istanbul *(page 45)*

Grand Bazaar The largest covered market in the world with 4,000 shops *(page 43)*

Ephesus One of the best-preserved ancient sites in Turkey and the top historical attraction along the Aegean coast *(page 79)*

Janissary Band concert Reviving days of Ottoman glory in spectacular fashion *(page 59)*

Topkapı Palace Richly adorned home of the sultans and their harem *(page 32)*

Basilica Cistern Part of the city's Byzantine-era system of underground reservoirs *(page 42)*

Aya Sofya Completed in AD537 and still one of the world's greatest architectural wonders *(page 28)*

İstiklal Caddesi At the heart of the lively, European-style New City *(page 56)*

CONTENTS

24

86

68

INTRODUCTION

Istanbul is one of the world's most venerable cities. Part of the city's allure is its setting, where Europe faces Asia across the waters of the Bosphorus, making it the only city in the world to bridge two continents.

Here, where the Black Sea blends into the Aegean, East and West mingle and merge in the cultural melting pot of Turkey's largest metropolis. Busy Oriental bazaars co-exist with European shops; kebab shops and coffee houses sit alongside international restaurants; modern office buildings and hotels alternate with Ottoman minarets along the city's skyline; traditional music and Western pop, belly-dancing and ballet, Turkish wrestling and football all compete for the attention of the *İstanbullu* audience.

This is the only city in the world to have been the capital of both an Islamic and a Christian empire. As Constantinople, jewel of the Byzantine Empire, it was for more than 1,000 years the most important city in Christendom. As Istanbul it was the seat of the Ottoman sultans, rulers of a 500-year Islamic empire that stretched from the Black Sea and the Balkans to Arabia and Algeria.

Strategic Location

Istanbul owes its long-held historical significance to a strategic location at the mouth of the Bosphorus. From this vantage point the city could control not only the ships that passed through the strait on the important trade route between the Black Sea and the Mediterranean, but also the overland traffic travelling from Europe into Asia Minor, which used the narrow strait as a crossing point. In the words of the 16th-century French traveller Pierre Gilles: 'The Bosphorus with one key opens and closes two worlds, two seas.'

Talking Turkey

The name Turkey relates to both a country and Christmas or thanksgiving dinner. Is there some relationship? The succulent birds we enjoy at these festivals originated in the Americas. Turks call a turkey a 'hindi' though. Certainly, the Moghul Emperor Jahangir had a painting of a turkey – perhaps he imported them and exported them to Turkey and thus to Europe.

That strategic advantage is no less important today than it was 2,500 years ago, when a band of Greeks first founded the city of Byzantium on this very spot. Ankara may be the official capital of modern Turkey, but Istanbul remains the country's largest city, most important commercial and industrial centre, and busiest port, accounting for more than one-third of Turkey's manufacturing output.

The Bosphorus is one of the world's most active shipping lanes, and the overland traffic is now carried by two of the world's longest suspension bridges.

Urban Contrasts

The thriving city has long since spread beyond the 5th-century Byzantine walls built by Emperor Theodosius II and now sprawls for miles along the shores of the Sea of Marmara on both the European and Asian sides. Back in 1507 this was the world's largest city, with a population of 1.2 million. That figure has now passed 12 million and is still growing, swollen by a steady influx of people from rural areas (more than half the population was born in the provinces). These new arrivals have created a series of shantytowns around the perimeter of the city. Their makeshift homes, known in Turkish as *gecekondu* ('built by night'), take advantage of an old Ottoman law that protects a house whose roof has been built during the hours of darkness. The slums are eventually knocked down to make way for new tower-blocks – a new suburb is created, yet another shantytown springs up beyond it, and Istanbul spreads out a little farther.

At the other end of the social spectrum are the wealthy İstanbullus, who live in the upmarket districts of Taksim, Harbiye and Nişantaşı, where the streets are lined with fashion boutiques, expensive apartments and stylish cafés. Those belonging to this set are the lucky few who frequent the city's more expensive restaurants and casinos, and retire at the weekends to their *yalı* (restored wooden mansions) along the Bosphorus. But most of Istanbul's inhabitants fall between these two extremes, living in modest flats and earning an average wage in the offices, shops, banks and factories that provide most of the city's employment.

Reviving the past: on parade with the Janissary Band

Although small Armenian, Greek Orthodox, Jewish and Catholic communities survive, the majority of İstanbullus are Muslim and adhere to the principles known as the 'Five Pillars of Islam' – to believe with all one's heart that 'There is no God but God, and Mohammed is his Prophet'; to pray five times a day, at dawn, midday, afternoon, sunset and after dark; to give alms to the poor and towards the upkeep of the mosques; to fast between sunrise and sunset during the month of Ramadan; and

Entering the Blue Mosque

to try to make the pilgrimage to Mecca at least once in one's lifetime.

Islam in Turkey is, on the whole, an open, welcoming brand of the religion, where the visitor is made to feel at home (in being able to go into mosques, for example). The secular society created by Atatürk is clearly visible in the contemporary culture and fashion followed by both men and women, but there is creeping conservatism among the poor, who look to Islam to solve their economic problems. Government is strictly secular, a principle strongly guarded by the military.

Principal Attractions

Just as the Bosphorus separates Asia from Europe, so the inlet called the Golden Horn separates the old Istanbul from the new. The main attractions for the visitor are concentrated in the historic heart of old Istanbul. Three great civilisations have shaped this part of the city – Roman, Byzantine and Ottoman. Though little remains from Roman times, the city's Byzantine legacy boasts Aya Sofya (the Church of the Divine Wisdom), one of the world's greatest buildings; the magnificent mosaics of St Saviour in Chora; and the impressive Theodosian Walls. The Ottomans built countless mosques in their capital, the finest of which is the Süleymaniye, built by Turkey's greatest architect, Sinan. But the most popular tourist sight is Topkapı Palace, the home of the Ottoman sultans, where the riches of the Imperial Treasury and the intrigue of the Harem draw many thousands of visitors each year.

From the belvedere in the treasury of the palace, where the Sultan used to gaze down upon his fleet, you can look across the mouth of the Golden Horn to the modern district of Beyoğlu, where multi-storey hotels rise beyond the turret of the Galata Tower. Round the corner, by the Bosphorus, is the glittering façade of the 19th-century Dolmabahçe Palace, while beyond stretches the span of the Bosphorus Bridge, a concrete symbol of the city, linking Europe with Asia.

Byzantium, Constantinople, Istanbul – down the centuries the city has been open to influences from both East and West, and this cross-fertilisation of ideas has created one of the world's liveliest, most engaging and most hospitable cultures. It is neither European nor Oriental, but an unparalleled and intoxicating blend; it is, quite simply, unique.

Dolmabahçe Palace, viewed from the Bosphorus

A BRIEF HISTORY

Byzas, the legendary founder of Byzantium, was the son of the sea god Poseidon. His maternal grandfather was Zeus. In around 660BC, the oracle at Delphi told him to settle an area opposite some blind people who had established a town on the eastern shore of the Bosphorus. They must have been blind not to have noticed the advantages of such a site: surrounded by water on three sides, it not only occupied a perfect strategic location, but was an ideal spot for trade. The Topkapı Palace, transport hubs and bazaars occupy the same position today.

Ford of the ox

The name Bosphorus stems from Greek mythology: the King of the Gods, Zeus, fell for Io, but his wife Hera wasn't pleased. Poor Io was turned into a cow, goaded so sorely by a gadfly that she swam the Bosphorus, the ford of the ox.

Centuries earlier, Jason and the Argonauts, seeking the Golden Fleece, had rowed through the Bosphorus following a pigeon, and escaped the clashing rocks, which threatened to kill them. The rocks never clashed again. Could this myth have grown from an earthquake, which are common here?

The shores of the Aegean are equally fabled. The Trojan War stemmed from the love of Paris for Helen of Troy. The ancient Greeks took the fall of Troy, as recounted by Homer, as the starting point of their history.

Aegean Cities

The Mycenaean Greeks who conquered King Priam's Troy soon lost their homelands. Power changes forced successive waves of immigration: the Ionians and others settled on the Turkish shore. While Greece went into a 'Dark Age', civilisation blossomed here. By the 8th century BC the 12 main city-states of Ionia, including Ephesus, Priene and Miletus, had formed what was known as the Pan-Ionic League. Science, philosophy, architecture and the arts flourished, and the Ionians founded further colonies.

In the 6th century BC coastal city-states fell to the Persians, who incorporated them into their empire. Athens supported a revolt, which was quickly subdued. Athenian involvement provoked the Persian King Darius to invade the Greek mainland. He suffered a succession of defeats: the famous Battle of Marathon in 490BC and the loss of the Persian fleet at the Battle of Salamis 10 years later.

Ancient ruins at Priene

As a result of the Persian Wars, cities along the Aegean coast were encouraged to join the Delian Confederacy, paying tribute to Athens in return for protection against the Persians. Athens demanded this source of easy money and dissent soon grew among the member cities. There followed the Peloponnesian War (431–404BC) after which Sparta led the confederacy. The Persians, sensing weakness in the ranks, launched another offensive, resulting in the Aegean coast cities coming under Persian control in 387BC.

Alexander the Great

Meanwhile, King Philip II of Macedon dreamed of driving the Persians out of northern Greece and unifying the entire Greek world. He thought Byzantium was well positioned and attempted to take it in 340BC.

Philip's dreams were surpassed by his son Alexander the Great, who lived for only 33 years (356–323BC). In 334BC, aged 22, he led his army across the Hellespont (now the Dardanelles). He paused at Troy to make a sacrifice at the Temple of Athena and pay homage to his hero Achilles, before going on to defeat the Persians. Having conquered the Aegean and Mediterranean coasts of Anatolia, and subdued Syria and Egypt, Alexander took the great prize of Persepolis, the Persian capital, before advancing into India. He built the greatest empire the world had yet seen, although it lasted only 10 years.

After Alexander's death, his empire was divided among his generals. The conflict between them left the Turkish Aegean and Byzantium open to acquisition by Rome.

Enter the Romans

Attalus III, the last of the Attalid kings, a dynasty dating from 264BC, ruled a prosperous city-state, Pergamon, on the Aegean. When he died in 133BC, his subjects discovered that he had bequeathed his kingdom to the Romans. Thus Pergamon became the capital of the new Roman province of Asia. Under Emperor Augustus, Rome ceased to be a republic, and, in 27BC, became an empire. There followed a long period of peace and prosperity known as the Pax Romana. Asia Minor (the Roman name for Anatolia) was incorporated

The Crescent Moon

Philip of Macedon launched his raid on Byzantium in the dead of night. But the goddess of the moon, Hecate, illuminated the scene and foiled Philip's plot. This divine intervention was commemorated by the striking of coins bearing her star and crescent. Some say that's why the crescent moon became an important symbol, later passed on to the Ottomans and, subsequently, to the Islamic world.

into the Roman Empire. The advent of Christianity threatened the Roman establishment because it rejected the old gods and denied the divinity of the emperor. The journeys of St Paul the Apostle (AD40 to 56) led to the founding of many churches, notably the Seven Churches of Asia addressed in the Revelation of St John – Pergamon, Smyrna, Ephesus, Thyatira, Laodicea, Sardis and Philadelphia.

Theodosian Walls

City of Constantine

Meanwhile Byzantium had developed as a city-state, much like the cities of the Aegean. It, too, fell under the sway of Athens, Sparta, Persia, Alexander and Rome. It tried to regain its independence from Rome, but proved too small and weak, and was conquered by Emperor Septimius Severus in AD196. He had the city razed to the ground, but then saw the advantages of its strategic location, and began a programme of enlarging and strengthening the old defensive walls.

Weak and decadent emperors saw the Roman Empire decline into anarchy. In AD286 Diocletian sought to reverse the decline by splitting the administration of the empire in two. His policy succeeded for a time, but following his abdication in AD305, the empire continued to weaken, harassed by invaders and troubled by internal strife.

Constantine the Great (who was a convert to Christianity) reunited the empire. He chose Byzantium as his new capital to emphasise the break with heathen Rome. The city was

Haghia Sophia mosaic

inaugurated with great ceremony in AD330 and, in honour of the emperor, was renamed Constantinople. Constantine added new city walls, following a plan he claimed to have been given by Christ in a vision, and commissioned many monuments including a grand central forum decorated with a triumphal column. The 'New Rome' soon achieved a pre-eminence in the Christian world that it would retain for 1,000 years.

In 392 the Emperor Theodosius proclaimed Christianity to be the official religion of the Roman Empire. On his death in 395 the empire was split once more, between his two sons. The Western Empire, ruled from Rome, fell in 476, but the Eastern, or Byzantine Empire, became one of the longest-lived empires the world has ever known, dating from 395 to 1453. The greatest of the Byzantine emperors was Justinian (527–65), who extended the boundaries of the empire into Spain, Italy and Africa. Together with his wife, Theodora, he encouraged the arts, reformed the legal system, and commissioned the building of the magnificent basilica, the Haghia Sophia (Aya Sofya).

Crusades

Following the death of the Prophet Mohammed in 632, Arab armies, united under Islam, took Egypt, Syria and Palestine from the Byzantines; Constantinople was besieged from 674 to 678, but survived because of its defences. North Africa and Italy were lost. Troubled times were only lightened by a brief golden age under Basil II (976–1025) before further invasions by the Seljuk Turks came to wrest large parts of Asia Minor from Constantinople's control. Christian holy places were threatened and pilgrims bound for Jerusalem attacked.

Emperor Alexius Commenus had sought help from the Christian West to recover his lost territory, but got more than he bargained for as the 'barbarian' Franks of the First Crusade rampaged across the region and finally captured Jerusalem in 1099 (massacring Muslims and Jews as well as local Christians in the process). However, the Second and Third Crusades were a disaster for the Christians. The Fourth Crusade, launched in 1202 and partly inspired by Venetian jealousy of Byzantium's trading power, became an excuse to plunder Constantinople itself. Thus, the city that had held out against so many attacks by the infidel became subjected to mindless pillaging by fellow Christians. Constantinople was recaptured in 1261, but the city had been shattered and its great monuments were stripped of gold, silver and precious works of art. The place was never the same again.

Crusaders sack Constantinople

Ottoman Rule

The Turks in Anatolia rallied under the banner of Sultan Osman Gazi, who defeated the Byzantines in 1300. By the 15th century, the whole

Süleyman the Magnificent

of Anatolia and Thrace, except for Constantinople, was under the control of these Osmanli (or Ottoman) Turks. The Byzantine emperor at the time, Manuel II (1391–1425), attempted to appease his enemies by allowing a Turkish district, mosque and tribunal within his city, and by courting Turkish goodwill with gifts of gold, but to no avail. The young Ottoman Sultan, Mehmet II, who reigned from 1451 to 1481, set about cutting off Constantinople's supply lines. The huge fortress of Rumeli Hisarı on the Bosphorus was built in just four months in 1452.

The Byzantines tried to protect the Golden Horn from enemy ships by stretching a huge chain across its mouth. They strengthened the city walls that had saved them so many times in the past, and waited for the inevitable onslaught. In April 1453 the Sultan's armies massed outside the walls, outnumbering the Byzantines 10 to one. The siege lasted seven weeks. The Ottoman admiral bypassed the defensive chain by having his ships dragged overland under cover of darkness. The final assault came on 29 May 1453, when the Ottoman army surged through a breach in the walls. The last emperor, Constantine XI, fell in the fighting, and by noon that day Mehmet and his men had taken control of the city.

After allowing his soldiers three days of pillaging, he restored order, acting with considerable leniency and good sense. Henceforth he became known as 'Fatih' (conqueror), and his newly won capital was renamed Istanbul. Mehmet ordered that Haghia Sophia be converted into a mosque; on the following Friday, he attended the first Muslim prayers in what came to be called Aya Sofya Camii (Mosque of Aya Sofya).

Mehmet laid claim to all the territories previously held by the Byzantines. Expansion continued and during the reign of his great grandson, Süleyman, the Ottoman Empire reached its greatest and most celebrated heights. Süleyman the Magnificent, aged 25, ascended the throne and ruled for 46 years (1520–66), the longest and most glorious reign in the history of the Ottomans. Istanbul was ornamented by the new rulers with elegant, richly decorated buildings, mosques and palaces, public buildings and fountains. This was the period of the master architect, Sinan, whose most famous work is the Süleymaniye Mosque.

Imperial expansion continued and by the mid-17th century the Ottoman Empire stretched from the eastern end of the Black Sea to Algeria, taking in Mesopotamia, Palestine, the shores of the Red Sea (including Mecca and Medina), Egypt, Anatolia, Greece, the Balkans, Hungary, Moldavia, the North African coast, the Crimea and southern Ukraine.

Sinan

Sinan (1489–1588) was the most celebrated Ottoman architect. Before taking up the profession (at the age of 49), he worked as a construction officer in the Janissary corps of the army. He designed hundreds of buildings, but is best remembered for his mosques, which include the Sehzade and Süleymaniye mosques in Istanbul and the Selimiye Mosque in Edirne. The basic template for his designs was Aya Sofya (completed AD537), but he refined the use of domes, half domes and buttresses both to maximise interior space and to achieve the best natural lighting on the richly decorated interior surfaces.

Atatürk

Decline and Fall

Such far-flung territories made effective rule impossible, and years of decadence, bitter family infighting that led to the premature deaths of most of the Ottomans with leadership qualities, and intermittent wars caused the sultanate to fall into irreversible decline. The failure of the siege of Vienna in 1683 highlighted the weakening. The Istanbul court was still elegant: Ahmet III presided over festivities from 1703 until he was deposed in 1730. Gradually the sultans moved further and further into European control, bringing in foreigners to advise on, then run, every aspect of the Empire.

The massacre of the Janissaries (the elite corps of the Ottoman army) in the Hippodrome in 1826 opened the door to change, ridding the court of its standing army. It is estimated that 10,000 were slain. Ottoman garb was replaced by Prussian blue uniforms, and the Ottoman Topkapı was replaced by the rococo Dolmabahçe Palace. But attempts at reform came too late; by 1876 the government was bankrupt. Sultan Abdül Hamid II (1876–1909) tried to apply absolute rule, and succeeded only in creating discontent amongst the younger generation of educated Turks who were increasingly interested in Western ways of government and social organisation. The Galatasaray Lycée (French Academy) and Anglophone colleges were turning out young men with dreams of democracy. These intellectuals formed an underground group known as the 'Young Turks'. In

1909, their revolt removed Abdül Hamid and replaced him with his brother, Mehmet V.

There followed the Balkan Wars, and World War I, into which Turkey entered on Germany's side. In the notorious Gallipoli campaign of 1915, the Turks, under the leadership of General Mustafa Kemal, defeated the Allied attack on the Dardanelles. At the end of the war, the Treaty of Sèvres stripped the Ottoman Empire of its lands, which were divided between the various Allied powers.

Atatürk and the Turkish Republic

In 1920, Mustafa Kemal was elected president of the Grand National Assembly in Ankara in defiance of the Sultan's government in Constantinople. He was a war leader and popular politician, and set about turning defeat into victory as he ruthlessly liberated Turkey of its foreign invaders, and its more troublesome people, such as the Armenians. He had the delicate task of abolishing the sultanate without antagonising religious elements (the Sultan was also the caliph, leader of the Islamic world). In 1922, Mehmet VI, last of the Ottoman sultans, finally went into exile.

From 1925 to 1935, Kemal transformed the country. He secularised institutions, reformed the calendar, adapted the Latin alphabet for the Turkish language, emancipated women, outlawed Dervishes and improved industry and agriculture. He was enormously popular with the common Turkish people, and after he died in 1938, thousands lined the railway track

Name change

Atatürk introduced the Western idea of surnames (until then Turks had a single name) and made everyone choose a family name, which they had to hand down to their children. For himself he chose Atatürk, or Father of the Turks. It proved appropriate, as he almost single-handedly created the modern Turkish state.

The Turkish flag over Topkapı

to salute the white presidential train as it carried him from Istanbul for burial in Ankara, the new capital.

In 1923 Ankara had been made the capital of Turkey. It was a clean break with the past. The diplomats abandoned the Rue de Pera, which was renamed İstiklal Caddesi (Avenue of Independence). Istanbul lost revenues and status, and the city was left with its imperial past and an uncertain future.

Istanbul – at Last

The 1930s were the romantic 'Orient Express' years celebrated by foreign writers at the Pera Palas Hotel, but the 1940s were depressing, blighted by corruption and depopulation.

Since the war, Turkey has had mixed fortunes both economically and politically, with the military often on hand to safeguard Atatürk's legacy from economic and social disorder or from militant Islamist forces. But Istanbul seems to have ploughed on regardless, and since the 1960s, when major transport and restoration schemes were set in motion, its revival has been spectacular. The city has re-established itself as the hub of the nation's cultural life and the powerhouse of its economy, with the largest companies and banks, the main national newspapers, television networks and advertising agencies all having their headquarters here. Clean and efficiently run, Istanbul is back in the top league of world cities, and certainly won't be bowed by the kind of terrorist attacks to which it periodically falls victim.

Historical Landmarks

circa **660BC** Byzantium founded by Byzas the Greek.

AD196 City razed to ground by Septimius Severus.

330 Constantine makes Byzantium the new capital of his empire.

395 Death of Theodosius I; final division of Roman Empire.

413–447 Theodosius II builds new city walls.

527–565 Reign of Justinian the Great.

532–537 Construction of Haghia Sophia (Aya Sofya).

726–843 Iconoclastic Crisis divides the empire.

11th century Seljuk Turks invade Asia Minor.

1204–61 Crusaders sack Constantinople and occupy the city.

1326 The Osmanli Turks capture Bursa; the Ottoman Empire is born.

1453 Mehmet the Conqueror captures Constantinople and makes it his capital, renamed Istanbul.

1520–66 Reign of Süleyman the Magnificent.

1683 Ottoman Empire reaches its greatest extent.

18th century Ottomans lose territory to European powers.

1826 Massacre of the Janissaries in the Hippodrome.

1909 Young Turks depose Sultan Abdül Hamid II.

1915 The Turks under Mustafa Kemal (Atatürk) defeat the Allied attack on the Dardanelles.

1922 The sultanate is abolished.

1923 Turkey becomes a republic; Atatürk elected president.

1938 Death of Atatürk.

1952 Turkey joins NATO.

1973 Bosphorus Bridge completed.

1999 Earthquake hits the Istanbul area.

2001 onwards Tourism to Turkey temporarily slumps after 9/11.

2003 onwards The city is rocked by sporadic terrorist attacks carried out by both Kurdish separatist and extreme Islamist groups.

2005 Negotiations on Turkey joining the European Union begin.

2007 After a standoff between secularists and Islamists over the choice of the next president, the ruling AK Party wins parliamentary elections.

WHERE TO GO

Modern Istanbul is split in two by the narrow, sinuous strait known as the Bosphorus. The mood varies in different areas of the city. Sultanahmet, the heart of the Old City, has the excitement of distinctive architecture – there's so much to see, and you know that you are in the Orient. Towards the city walls, Fatih is conservative and poorer.

Across the Galata Bridge, the feeling is more cosmopolitan, but with hints of a naughty, fin-de-siècle, Art Nouveau history. Taksim Square is much like any main square in any big city, full of traffic and people in a hurry. The Asian side of the city is contrary to stereotypes, as it is altogether more modern, organised and rich.

This guide takes Eminönü as the starting point for tours of Istanbul. It is possible to reach almost all of the city's attractions from this central point using public transport. The transport system is efficient and easy to use. Eminönü is the terminus for the *feribot* (ferries); and nearby Sirkeci Station is the European railway terminus, where the Orient Express used to steam in, trailing romance and drama in its path. Nowadays, the travellers are mostly suburban commuters, but the station has had a bit of a facelift and is worth a look with a good restaurant and a small museum detailing its romantic past. (Asian trains leave from the Haydarpaşa Station across the Bosphorus.)

Take the tram

A tram line runs past the Dolmabahçe to Eminönü, across the Galata Bridge, through Sultanahmet, past the Grand Bazaar, the hotels of Laleli and Aksaray, and on to the city walls at Topkapı bus station (not to be confused with the famous palace of the same name). It is a handy way of getting from one sight to another.

Inside the Spice Bazaar

THE OLD CITY (STAMBOUL)

Eminönü

Istanbul's most popular tourist attractions are concentrated in the Sultanahmet district, but before setting out there are sights to be seen in Eminönü. At rush hour the waterfront becomes a bedlam of bodies as commuters pour off the ferries from the New City or the Asian side. The air is loud with blasts from ships' horns, and the water boils white as half-a-dozen vessels jostle for a vacant berth. Smaller boats equipped with cooking fires and frying pans bounce around in the wash, while their crews dish up mackerel sandwiches to hungry workers standing on the quayside, seemingly oblivious to the violent, churning movement of their floating kitchens. Adding to the activity are the sellers of grilled corn-cobs and fried mussels, who compete with the kitchen boats for passing trade.

The wide square opposite the Galata Bridge is dominated by the **New Mosque** *(Yeni Camii)*. Commissioned in 1597 by the Valide Sultan Safiye, mother of Mehmet III, it was not completed until 1663, making the Yeni Camii the youngest of Istanbul's classical mosques.

The large archway to the right of the mosque is the entrance to the famous **Spice Bazaar,** also known as the Egyptian Bazaar *(Mısır Çarşısı)*. It was opened a few years before the Yeni Camii, and its revenues originally paid for repairs to the mosque complex. Inside, the air is heady with the mingled aromas of ginger, pepper, cinnamon, cloves and freshly ground coffee. The L-shaped building has 88 shops, many still devoted to the sale of spices, herbs and herbal remedies, but dried fruit and nuts, *lokum* (Turkish Delight), fresh fruit and flowers, apple tea, and souvenirs occupy most stalls, although the stalls in the nearby streets sell more mundane household items.

If you leave the Spice Bazaar by the gate at the far end of the first aisle and then turn right, you will find the **Mosque of Rüstem Paşa** *(Rüstempaşa Camii)*, with its minaret soaring above the narrow backstreet. This is one of Sinan's smaller works, and one of his most beautiful. The interior is almost completely covered in İznik tiles of the finest period, with floral and geometric designs in blue, turquoise and coral red.

The Spice of Life

At the Spice Bazaar in Eminönü, sellers once sat cross-legged on carpets, ready to seize pestle and mortar for pounding potions both efficacious and fanciful, optimistically prepared to cure anything from lumbago to lovesickness through to highly complicated cases of combatting the Evil Eye. Nor were they all charlatans – some of the market's herbal remedies are still available, even though they no longer contain such rare (or interesting) ingredients as ambergris, dragon's blood or tortoise eggs.

Aya Sofya

Sultanahmet

Sultanahmet occupies the summit of the first of the Old City's seven hills. This was the site of the original Byzantium, founded in the 7th century BC, and of the civic centre of Constantinople, capital of the Byzantine Empire. Here, too, the conquering Ottoman sultans chose to build their most magnificent palaces and mosques.

Aya Sofya

Of the few remains of the Byzantine city, the most remarkable building is **Aya Sofya** (also known as Haghia Sophia; open Tues–Sun 9.30am–4.30pm, Jun–Oct 9am–7pm; admission fee). For almost 1,000 years, this was the greatest church in Christendom, an architectural wonder built by the Byzantine Empire to impress the world.

It is thought that a Christian basilica was built here in AD325 by Emperor Constantine, on the site of a pagan temple. It was destroyed by fire in AD404 and rebuilt by Theodosius II, then burnt down again in 532. The building you see today was commissioned by Justinian and completed in 537, although many repairs, additions and alterations have been made over the centuries. The dome was damaged by earthquakes several times, and the supporting buttresses have coarsened the church's outward appearance.

The finest materials were used in its construction – white marble from the islands of the Marmara, *verd antique* from Thessaly, yellow marble from Africa, gold and silver from Ephesus, and ancient red porphyry columns that possibly came from Egypt and may once have stood in the Temple of the Sun at Baalbek. The interior was covered with golden mosaics, lit by countless flickering candelabras.

The last Christian service ever to be held in Haghia Sophia took place on 28 May 1453, the day before Constantinople fell to the Turks. Mehmet the Conqueror immediately converted the building to an imperial mosque, and built a brick minaret at the southeast corner. The architect, Sinan, strengthened the buttresses and added the other three minarets during the 16th century. Aya Sofya served as a mosque until 1935, when Atatürk proclaimed that it should become a museum.

The entrance path leads past the ticket desk to a shady tea-garden outside the main portal, which is surrounded by architectural fragments from the 5th-century church built by Theodosius; an excavated area to the left of the door reveals a part of this earlier building. You enter the building through the central portal, across a worn and well-polished threshold of *verd antique* and under a 9th-century mosaic of Christ Pantocrator, into the long, narrow narthex, running to right and left. Note the beautiful matching panels of marble, and the vaulted gold mosaic ceiling.

The cavernous interior

As you continue through the huge bronze doors of the Imperial Gate, your eyes will be drawn skywards by the upwards sweep of the dome. The scale is overwhelming: the dome is around 31m (100ft) in diameter, and floats 55m (180ft) above the floor – the same height as a 15-storey building.

The sensation of space is created by the absence of supporting walls beneath the dome. It was the great achievement of the architects Isidorus and Anthemius to transfer the weight of the dome to the pillars using semi-domes, arches and pendentives (the four triangular sections of masonry that fill the gaps between arches and dome) to create the illusion of an unsupported dome.

The original decoration has long since disappeared. Eight huge medallions, bearing the Arabic names of Allah, Mohammed, two of his grandsons and the first four caliphs, and a quotation from the Koran in the crown of the dome, are remnants of Aya Sofya's 500 years of service as an imperial mosque, as are the elaborate *mihrab* and *mimber* in the apse. But a few Christian **mosaics** survive – above the apse is the Virgin with the infant Jesus, with the Archangel Gabriel to the right (his companion Michael, to the left, has vanished save for a few feathers from his wings).

The best mosaics are in the galleries, reached by a spiral ramp that starts at the north end of the narthex. By the south wall is the famous **Deesis**, an extraordinary 13th-century mosaic showing Christ flanked by the Virgin Mary and St John the Baptist. On the east wall are two images showing Byzantine emperors and empresses making offerings to Christ on his throne (to the left) and to the Virgin and Child.

At the east end of the galleries, two small columns and a circle of green marble mark the spot where the empress sat during services; on the floor of the nave below, a circle of coloured stone to the right of centre is the **Opus Alexandrinum**, the place where the Byzantine emperors were crowned.

As you leave by the door at the south end of the narthex, turn around and look up to see a beautiful 10th-century **mosaic** of an emperor and empress offering symbols of Haghia Sophia and Constantinople to the Virgin Mary and Child.

Weeping Column

While inside Aya Sofya, look for the Weeping Column, also known as the Column of St Gregory. It has a thumb-sized hole covered with a brass plate. When you insert a finger, it comes out damp – the moisture is said to have healing powers, especially for eye diseases.

Topkapı Palace (Topkapı Sarayı)

Between Aya Sofya and the tip of Saray Burnu is the walled enclosure of **Topkapı Palace** (open Wed–Mon 9.30am–5pm, Jun–Oct 9am–7pm; admission fee, separate admission for Treasury and Harem), the former residence and seat of government of the Ottoman sultans. Begun in 1462 by Mehmet the Conqueror, it was extended by each succeeding sultan until it became a miniature city, which included mosques, libraries, stables, kitchens, schools, the imperial mint, treasuries, barracks, armouries, government offices, and audience halls. At its height it supported a population of nearly 4,000.

Sultan Abdül Mecit moved into the newly built Dolmabahçe Palace in 1853 *(see page 59)*, and by 1909 Topkapı was completely abandoned. In 1924 it was converted into a museum, and has been undergoing a continuous programme of restoration ever since. It is the city's most popular tourist attraction, and deserves a full day to do it justice. If pushed for time, the 'must-sees' are, in order of importance, the Harem (go early, get a timed ticket and see the rest while you wait), the Treasury and the Pavilion of the Holy Mantle.

Topkapı – the Film

Fans of 'exotic' locales will appreciate Jules Dassin's *Topkapı* (1964). The film has some wonderful scenes of Istanbul, including the old wooden houses that used to be such a feature of the city, and some of which still stand, in various states of repair, around the Topkapı Palace. The star was Dassin's wife, Melina Mercouri. In the film, she gets her boyfriend (Maximillian Schell) to assemble a team to pull off a heist – stealing the Topkapı dagger with its wonderful emeralds. The action is terrific, and there's a lengthy sequence featuring oiled wrestling. The film is made by the presence of Peter Ustinov, who won an Oscar for his performance as a bumbling Brit, and Akim Tamiroff, as a foul-mouthed, drunken cook.

The palace is laid out as a series of courtyards linked by ceremonial gates. You enter through the **Imperial Gate** (built in 1478) into the wooded gardens of the First Court. On the left is the Byzantine church of **Haghia Eirene** (Divine Peace), re-built together with Haghia Sophia after being burnt down in 532 (open only for concerts and events). This area was also known as the **Court of the Janissaries**, after the crack military corps that served as the sultan's bodyguard and used it as an assembly ground while on duty at the palace (the name derives from the Turkish *yeni çeri*, meaning 'new army'). It

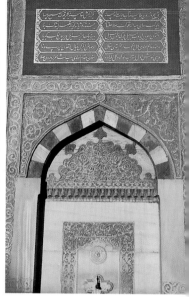

Detail of the fountain outside the Imperial Gate

originally contained the palace bakery, the armoury and the mint. At the far right-hand corner is the ticket office, which originally served as a prison. The fountain is called the Executioner's Fountain because here he rinsed his sword and washed his hands after carrying out his orders; examples of his handiwork were displayed on pikes at the Imperial Gate.

Buy your ticket and pass through the turreted Gate of Salutations, better known as the Orta Kapı, or **Middle Gate**. Only the sultan was permitted to ride through this gate on horseback; all others had to dismount and bow. It leads into the Second Court, also known as the **Court of the Divan** because the Imperial Council (known as the Divan) governed the Ottoman

Divan Tower

Empire from here. Five avenues radiate from the inside of the gate. To the right lie the **Palace Kitchens**, housing a collection of European crystal, Chinese porcelain, and Ottoman serving dishes and cooking implements. Straight ahead is the ornate Gate of the White Eunuchs, which leads into the Third Court *(see page 36)*. The avenue on the left leads towards the pointed **Divan Tower** *(Divan Kulesi)*, at the foot of which lie the Council Chamber and the Grand Vezir's Office.

Here, too, is the entrance to Topkapı's main attraction, the **Harem** (open 10am–4pm, 30-minute guided tour only; additional ticket required). The Harem housed the private quarters of the sultan, his mother and his wives and concubines. Its network of staircases, corridors and courtyards linked the sumptuously decorated chambers of the royal household, and harboured a claustrophobic world of ambition, jealousy and intrigue. You enter by the **Carriage Gate**, where the women mounted their carriages. The only adult males allowed in the Harem were the Black Eunuchs, who were in charge of security and administration. Their quarters opened off the narrow **Courtyard of the Black Eunuchs**, beyond the gate. Windows in the colonnade on the left give a glimpse of their tiny rooms; sticks hanging on the walls were used to beat miscreants on the soles of their feet.

A long, narrow corridor lined with shelves (for trays of food) leads to the Courtyard of the Women Servants, from which you enter the **Apartments of the Valide Sultan** (the sultan's mother, who was the most powerful woman in the Harem). Her domed sitting room is panelled with 17th-century Kütahya tiles, and decorated with scenic views. A raised platform framed by two columns contains divans and a low dining table. The door on the left, beyond the hearth, leads to the valide sultan's bedchamber, with a gilded bed canopy and ornate floral faïence in turquoise, blue and red. A small adjoining prayer room has scenes of Mecca and Medina.

The right-hand door leads to the **Apartments of the Sultan** himself. First you pass the entrance to the royal bath chambers, designed by Sinan and richly ornamented in marble. There are paired but separate chambers for the sultan and the valide sultan, each having a changing room, a cool room and a hot room. The sultan was bathed by elderly female servants, then dried and pampered by groups of younger handmaidens.

Forbidden Fruits

The harem occupies an important place in Western fantasy. In fact, the word is derived from 'haram', meaning forbidden, and it was the place where the sultan and the women lived. Many women – wives and mothers – in the Islamic world had power and influence over their menfolk, but the harem women included 'odalisques', the slave girls who gripped the imagination of writers and artists – from Mozart and Balzac to Renoir and Picasso. Many famous artists produced paintings of girls they imagined, but there is little reality in the image. While Matisse was painting his odalisques, Atatürk was proclaiming the Turkish women's right to vote. When Picasso inherited the fascination from Matisse and began to paint odalisques, Turkish women had equal rights in many areas including education, and had had the franchise for 30 years.

Next, you enter the vast and splendid **Imperial Hall**, with three marble fountains, and a canopied throne from which the sultan would enjoy the music and dancing of his concubines. The even more splendid **Salon of Murat III** has inlaid floors, flowered İznik tiles, carved fountains, canopied sofas and a superb domed ceiling, designed by Sinan. On the far side a door leads to the Library of Ahmet I, with cupboard doors and shutters inlaid with mother-of-pearl and tortoiseshell, which in turn opens into the dining room of Ahmet III, better known as the **Fruit Room**. This tiny room is covered all over with lacquered paintings of flowers and fruit in rococo style. Ahmet III was known as the 'Tulip King', and celebrated each spring with a tulip festival in the palace grounds.

The exit from the Harem opens into the **Third Court**, otherwise reached through the Gate of the White Eunuchs. Inside the gate is the ornate **Throne Room** *(Arz Odası)*, where the sultan received foreign ambassadors. Head down to the right to the **Treasury** (additional ticket required), which contains an astonishing selection of artefacts and relics, chief among them the golden Topkapı Dagger, with three huge emeralds set in the hilt and a fourth forming the lid of a watch hidden in the handle; and the Spoonmaker's Diamond, an 86-carat, pear-shaped diamond set in a gold mount encrusted with 49 smaller diamonds. Exhibits include gilded thrones studded with precious stones, a pair of solid-gold candlesticks set with 666 diamonds (one for each verse of the Koran), and reliquaries containing the hand and part of the skull of John the Baptist.

Return to sender

The Persian emperor, Nadir Shah, sent the Ottoman emperor a jewelled throne. To return the complement, Istanbul dispatched the Topkapı dagger. But en route for Persia, the emissaries discovered that Nadir Shah had died, so they sensibly decided to hang onto the dagger and take it back home with them.

Across the courtyard is the magnificently decorated **Pavilion of the Holy Mantle**, which houses relics of the Prophet Mohammed (including hairs from his beard) and is therefore a place of great religious importance for Muslims. The **Fourth Court** contains a number of pretty pavilions and terraces, and a restaurant and cafeteria with fine views of the Bosphorus.

Pavilion of the Holy Mantle

Topkapı Museums

From Topkapı's First Court, a steep, narrow cobbled lane with finely restored Ottoman houses leads to the Fifth Court, which contains three excellent museums (open Tues–Sun 9.30am–5pm; single admission fee for all three; there is also an entry by Gulhane tram stop). The **Archaeological Museum** *(Arkeoloji Müzesi)* is one of the world's great collections, with galleries devoted to Cyprus, Syria and Palestine, the Phrygians, Troy and Anatolia, from the Palaeolithic to the Iron Age, as well as the classical era. Its main attraction is the magnificent collection of sarcophagi from Sidon (in modern Lebanon), especially the Alexander Sarcophagus, decorated with scenes of hunting and battle.

The **Museum of the Ancient Orient** *(Eski Şark Eserleri Müzesi)* displays objects from ancient Near and Middle Eastern civilisations, including Babylonian ceramic panels from the Ishtar Gates at the time of King Nebuchadnezzar (605–562BC),

Hittite stone sphinxes from Hattuşaş, the world's earliest known peace treaty, the Treaty of Kadesh, signed between the Hittites and Egyptians in 1269BC, and the oldest recorded set of laws, the Code of Hammurabi (1750BC).

Built in 1472 for Mehmet the Conqueror, and decorated with turquoise and blue tiles, the most eye-catching building in the square is the **Tiled Pavilion** *(Çinili Kösk)*. It houses a valuable display of ceramics going back to Seljuk times.

Hippodrome
The long arc that stretches southwest from Aya Sofya is known as the **Hippodrome** *(At Meydanı)*, and in Byzantine times that's exactly what it was. Inspired by the Circus Maximus in Rome, it was built in AD203 as a stadium for chariot-racing and other public events. Later it was enlarged by Constantine the Great and could hold an audience of 100,000.

Egyptian Obelisk

The Hippodrome was the setting for the ceremony that proclaimed Constantinople as the 'New Rome' in AD330, following the division of the Roman Empire, and soon became the civic centre of the Byzantine capital, decorated with imposing monuments and flanked by fine buildings. Unfortunately it was destroyed when the city was sacked during the Fourth

Crusade, and left stripped of its statues and marble seats. In the 17th century its ruins were used as a quarry for the building of the Blue Mosque (see page 40). Only its outline, a few brick vaults and three fine ancient monuments survive today.

The north end of the *spina*, or central axis, is marked by an ornate domed ablutions fountain, given to the city by Germany's Kaiser Wilhelm II to commemorate his visit in 1900. At the opposite end rise three remnants of the original Hippodrome. The **Egyptian Obelisk**, brought to Constantinople by Theodosius in AD390, had been commissioned by Pharaoh Thutmose III in the 16th century BC. What you see is only the top third of the original – it broke during shipment. The reliefs on the pedestal show Theodosius and his family in the Hippodrome presiding over the raising of the obelisk. The **Serpentine Column** consists of three intertwined bronze snakes; they originally supported a gold vase, but the snakes' heads and the vase have long since disappeared. It is the oldest Greek monument in Istanbul, commemorating the Greek victory over the Persians at Plataea in 479BC (it was brought here from Delphi by Constantine the Great). A second, deeply eroded stone obelisk is known as the **Column of Constantine Porphyrogenitus** as an inscription on its base records that the emperor of that name (AD913–59) had it restored and sheathed in gilded bronze plates.

Justinian's saviour

The Empress Theodora first appeared on stage at the Hippodrome as a dancing girl in a circus troupe. But perhaps her biggest role here came in January AD532, when she faced down an ugly riot between the rival Green and Blue political factions, known as the Nika Revolt. Buildings were set on fire and a new emperor proclaimed. As Justinian prepared to flee the city, the indomitable empress exhorted the troops to rally to his defence. Thirty thousand rioters were killed and the empire was saved.

Blue Mosque

The six minarets of the **Blue Mosque** dominate the skyline of the Hippodrome. Known in Turkish as the *Sultan Ahmet Camii* (Mosque of Sultan Ahmet), it was built between 1609 and 1616 for the Sultan Ahmet I, after which it became the city's principal imperial mosque because of its proximity to Topkapı Palace. To savour the full effect of the architect's skill, enter the courtyard through the gate which opens onto the Hippodrome. As you pass through the portal, the façade sweeps up in front of you in a fine crescendo of domes. (Go out through the door on the left of the courtyard to reach the entrance for tourists which leads to the mosque proper.)

Once inside you will see how the mosque earned its familiar name. The very air seems to be blue – more than 20,000 turquoise İznik tiles glow gently in the light from the mosque's 260 windows, decorated with lilies, carnations, tulips and

The Blue Mosque, with its six minarets and 16 balconies

roses. Four massive columns support a dome 22m (70ft) in diameter, and 43m (142ft) high at the crown – big, but not quite as big as Aya Sofya, the design of which obviously influenced the architect. The *mihrab* and *mimber* are of delicately carved white marble, and the ebony window shutters are inlaid with ivory

A rival for Mecca?

A mosque with six minarets is unusual. Apparently, the sultan wanted to outshine Aya Sofya but in doing so, he fell foul of those who felt that he was trying to vie with Mecca (which had six), and so he paid for a seventh minaret for Mecca.

and mother-of-pearl. The painted blue arabesques in the domes and upper walls are restorations; to see the originals, look at the wall beneath the sultan's loge.

Across from the Hippodrome and the Blue Mosque is the **Museum of Turkish and Islamic Arts** (*Türk ve İslam Eserleri Müzesi*; open Tues–Sun 9.30am–4.30pm; admission fee). The collection, housed in the former palace of Ibrahim Paşa, the son-in-law of Süleyman the Magnificent, includes illuminated Korans, inlaid Koran boxes, carpets, ceramics, and Persian miniatures. The ethnographic section has tableaux of a nomad tent, a yurt, a village house and a traditional carpet loom.

In the vaulted cellars beside the mosque the **Carpet and Kilim Museum** (*Hünkar Kasri*; closed for renovation) is a good place to see the finest antique carpets. For newer carpets look nearby in the **Hürrem Hamamı** (Baths of Roxelana; open Tues–Sat 9am–5.30pm), a bath house designed by Sinan in 1556 for the wife of Süleyman the Magnificent, now run as a government carpet shop. The Blue Mosque stands on the site of Constantine's palace, a treasury of 500 halls and 30 chapels. All that remains is the 6th-century mosaic floor, now housed in the **Mosaic Museum** (*Mozaik Müsezi*; open Wed–Mon 9am–4.30pm; admission fee). This is reached via the **Arasta Bazaar**, a small shopping mall of high-quality crafts shops.

Yerebatan Serayi

Yerebatan Sarayı

Across the tram lines from Aya Sofya lies the entrance to one of Istanbul's more unusual historic sights – the **Basilica Cistern**, also called the Sunken Palace (*Yerebatan Sarayı*; open daily 9am–4pm; admission fee). This amazing construction is part of the city's ancient system of underground reservoirs, which was fed by water from the Belgrade Forest. The cistern measures 140m (460ft) by 70m (230ft); its vaulted brick roof is supported by a forest of columns topped by Corinthian capitals, 336 in all, set in 12 rows of 28. It was built under Justinian in AD532 and used during the Byzantine era, but forgotten thereafter until 1545 when a Frenchman discovered that residents drew water from wells in their homes. He got into the cistern and it was brought back into use as the water supply for Topkapı. The cistern was restored and opened to visitors in 1987; as you make your way along the walkways between the columns you can marvel at the fact that it still stands, 1,500 years after it was built.

Çemberlitaş

The street with the tram lines that leads uphill from Sultanahmet is called **Divan Yolu**. It was (and still is) the main road leading to the city gates in Byzantine and Ottoman times. Just off the road, on Klodfarer Caddesi, the **Binbirdirek Sarnıcı** (the Cistern of 1001 Columns; open daily 9am–6pm for sightseeing, until midnight for eating; entrance fee refunded if you eat in the excellent restaurant) is an even older 4th-century cistern, with 264 columns – in spite of its name.

The next tram stop is called **Çemberlitaş** (Hooped Column) after the stone pillar that rises to the right of the road. Also called the **Burnt Column**, it was charred and cracked by a great fire that ravaged the district in 1770 (the iron hoops help to reinforce the column). Constantine erected it in AD330 to mark the city's new status as capital of the Eastern Roman Empire. Parts of the Cross and the nails with which Christ was crucified are reputed to be sealed in the column's base.

Built by Sinan, the **Çemberlitaş Hamamı** (Vezirhan Caddesi; open 6am–midnight) is still in use today as a Turkish bath and well worth a visit.

Inside the Grand Bazaar

The Grand Bazaar

Behind the Burnt Column rises the Baroque exterior of the **Nuruosmaniye Camii**, dating from 1755. Walk towards it, then turn left through an arched gate into the mosque precinct and follow the crowds into the bustling **Grand Bazaar**. The *Kapalı Çarşı* (Covered Market) of Istanbul is the world's largest covered bazaar, with about 4,000 shops, as well as banks, cafés, restaurants, mosques and a post office, crammed together in a grid of 66 narrow streets that total 8km (5 miles) in length – all protected from summer

The evil eye

You'll see many shops selling glass discs with a distinctive pattern of blue, white and black concentric circles. These are to avert the evil eye – it's as if they look back exclaiming, 'Yes! I've got my eye on you! I can see what you are up to!'

sun and winter rain by a multitude of domed and vaulted roofs. Mehmet the Conqueror built the first covered market on this site in 1461. It has been rebuilt several times after destruction by fire and earthquake.

Most of the streets follow a pattern and are well signposted. From the Nuruosmaniye entrance, stretching towards the **Beyazıt Gate**, is the main street, lined with jewellers' shops. On your right is the entrance to the 16th-century **Sandal Bedesten**, with brick vaults supported on stone pillars. It is quiet for most of the week, but comes alive during the auctions held here at 1pm on Tuesdays, Wednesdays and Thursdays. In the centre of the bazaar is the **Old Bedesten**, where you can find the best quality gold and silver jewellery, brass and copper ware, curios and antiques.

The Beyazıt Gate, at the far end of the main street *(Kalpakcılar Başı Caddesi)*, leads to a street of bargain clothing stalls. Turn right, and first left up the steps to the **Book Market** *(Sahaflar Çarşısı)*, a popular place for university folk.

Beyazıt

The next tram stop is **Beyazıt**. **Beyazıt Meydanı** is a vast, pigeon-thronged square below the entrance to Istanbul University. Site of the Roman Forum Tauri (Forum of the Bulls), it has been one of the city's main gathering points for 2,000 years. Over the weekend the square hosts a flea market, where vendors lay out a variety of new and second-hand goods. Old men sell bags of corn for you to feed to the pigeons, while brightly dressed water-sellers tout for business with cries of *'buz gibi!'* ('ice-cold!'), and encourage tourists to take a photograph – for a fee, of course.

The east side of the square is dominated by the beautiful **Beyazıt Camii**, built in the early 16th century by Sultan Beyazıt II, son of Mehmet the Conqueror. It is the earliest surviving example of classical Ottoman architecture, inspired by Aya Sofya *(see page 28)*. Opposite the mosque is the arched gateway to Istanbul University and the 50-m (148-ft) **Beyazıt Tower**, built in 1828 as a fire-lookout point.

The Süleymaniye

The outline of the Süleymaniye, the **Mosque of Süleyman the Magnificent**, rises from a site above the Golden Horn (near the north gate of Istanbul University). Deemed the finest Ottoman building in Istanbul, the mosque is a tribute to the 'Golden Age' of the Ottoman Empire, and to the two great men of

The Süleymaniye at sunset, from Eminönü

genius who created it – Sultan Süleyman I, the Magnificent, and his chief architect, Sinan. Süleyman, known in Turkish as Kanuni (The Lawgiver), reigned from 1520 to 1566, when the empire attained the height of its wealth and power.

The Süleymaniye and its complex of buildings were built between 1550 and 1557. Legend has it that jewels from Persia were ground up and mixed in with the mortar for one of the minarets, and that the incredible acoustics were achieved by embedding 64 hollow clay vessels facing neck-down in the dome. It is also said that Süleyman, in awe of his architect's achievement, handed the keys to Sinan at the inauguration ceremony and allowed him the privilege of opening it.

You enter through a courtyard, colonnaded with grand columns of granite, marble and porphyry, with a rectangular şadırvan (ablutions fountain) in the centre. The interior is vast and inspiring, flooded with light from the 16th-century stained-glass windows. The mosque is square in plan, about 58m (172ft) on each side, capped by a dome 27.5m (82ft) in diameter and 47m (140ft) high. The tiles are original İznik faïence, with floral designs; the woodwork of the doors and shutters is delicately inlaid with ivory and mother-of-pearl.

Both Süleyman and Sinan are buried nearby. The **tombs** of the sultan and his wife Roxelana (open daily 9.30am–4.30pm) lie behind the mosque in the walled garden, where roses and hollyhocks tangle among the tall grass between the gravestones, and sparrows swoop and squabble in the fig trees. Sinan's modest tomb (open Tues, Wed, Fri, Sun 9am–5pm), which he designed himself, stands in a triangular garden just outside the northern corner of the complex, capped by a small dome.

A walk around the terrace beside the mosque, which affords a fine view across the Golden Horn, will give you some idea of the huge size of the complex with its attendant soup kitchen and caravanserai, school and library, now housing restaurants and archives. The **hamam** is back in use (open 7am–midnight).

Towards the City Walls

The tram continues towards the city walls, passing Laleli and Aksaray, where there are many hotels, and out into the residential suburbs. There are a number of worthwhile sights between the Süleymaniye and the city walls, but they are scattered and you will want to use taxis to reach most of them. Away from the main roads, these mostly residential districts contain a maze of backstreets, muddy lanes and cobbled alleys. If you choose to walk, there are some good large-scale maps available. The odd, old wooden house that has survived the city's numerous fires leans creaking across the crumbling bricks of some forgotten Byzantine ruin.

One of Sinan's early buildings (1548) is the imposing **Şehzade Camii** (Mosque of the Prince), which now overlooks a park that is unfortunately spoilt by traffic noise. It was built in memory of Prince Mehmet, Süleyman the Magnificent's son, who died in 1543 aged 21.

The Aqueduct of Valens

Aqueduct of Valens

Spanning the park and the six lanes of the busy thoroughfare Atatürk Bulvarı are the impressive remains of the **Aqueduct of Valens** *(Bozdoğan Kemeri)*. First constructed in the 2nd century AD, it was rebuilt by Emperor Valens in the 4th century, restored several times by

Fish at a local market near Sultan Selim Camii

both the Byzantines and the Ottomans, and remained in use up to as recently as the 19th century.

If you follow the line of the aqueduct away from the city centre, you will soon reach the vast complex of the **Fatih Camii** (Mosque of the Conqueror), perched on top of the city's Fourth Hill. It was the first imperial mosque to be built following the Conquest of Constantinople in 1453, and its *külliye* (mosque complex), the biggest in the whole of the Ottoman Empire, included a hospital, poorhouses, a mental asylum, visitors' accommodation and a number of schools teaching science, mathematics, history and Koranic studies. Built by Mehmet the Conqueror between 1462 and 1470, the complex was almost completely destroyed by an earthquake in 1766. Only the courtyard and its huge portal survived; the rest was rebuilt. The tombs of the conqueror and his wife are in the walled graveyard behind the mosque.

Farther out, dominating the Fifth Hill, is the **Sultan Selim Camii** (Mosque of Selim I), dedicated to the father of Süleyman the Magnificent. Unlike its dedicatee, who was known as Yavuz Selim (Selim the Grim), the mosque is one of the most charming in the city, with a sparse but tasteful decoration of beautiful İznik tiles from the earliest period in turquoise, blue and yellow, and richly painted woodwork. Its dramatic situation overlooking the Golden Horn commands a fine, sweeping view across the picturesque districts of Fener and Balat.

Kariye Camii

The brightest jewel in Istanbul's Byzantine crown is the former church of **St Saviour in Chora**, known in Turkish as the **Kariye Camii** (open daily 9am–6.30pm, closed Wed; admission fee). Restored and opened as a museum in 1958, this small building, tucked away in a quiet corner of the city, is one of the world's greatest monuments to Byzantine art. The church's name means 'in the country' because the first one to be built on this site was outside the city walls. Although it was later enclosed within the Theodosian Walls, the name stuck.

The oldest part of the existing building, the central domed area, dates from 1120. The church was rebuilt and decorated early in the 14th century under the supervision of Theodore Metochites, an art-lover, statesman and scholar who was a friend and advisor of Emperor Andronicus II Palaeologus. Sadly, Metochites was reduced to poverty and sent into exile when the emperor was overthrown in 1328. He was allowed to return to the city in 1330 provided that he remained a monk at Chora, which he did, living out the last years of his life surrounded by the magnificent works of art he had commissioned.

St Saviour in Chora

Metochites left the central portion of the church intact, but he added the outer narthex and the pareclesion

Frescoes of the Apostles

(side chapel). The wonderful mosaics and frescoes, dating from between 1310 and 1320 (contemporary with those of Giotto in Italy), are almost certainly the work of a single artist, now unknown. Their subtlety of colour, liveliness of posture, and strong, lifelike faces record a last flowering of Byzantine art before its descent into decadence. The church was converted into a mosque in 1511, but fortunately it was not substantially altered. The mosaics were covered with wooden screens, some windows were boarded up, and a minaret was added.

The **mosaics** are grouped into four narrative cycles depicting the lives of Christ and the Virgin Mary, along with portraits of various saints, and large dedicatory panels. The mosaic above the door leading from the narthex into the nave shows the figure of Metochites, wearing a huge hat, offering a model of his beloved church to Christ. Each tiny tile is set at a different angle to its neighbours so that the reflected light creates the illusion of a shimmering, ethereal image. The **frescoes** are all in the parecclesion, which stretches the length of the building and was used in Byzantine times as a funerary chapel. The artist's masterpiece is the *Anastasis* (Resurrection) in the vault of the apse, showing Christ pulling Adam and Eve from their tombs, while the figure of Satan lies bound and helpless beneath His feet.

Fifteen minutes' walk from the Kariye, and marking the summit of the Sixth Hill, is the **Mihrimah Sultan Camii**, built by Sinan in 1565 for Süleyman's favourite daughter. Next to the mosque are the **Theodosian Walls**, pierced here by the **Adrianople Gate** *(Edirnekapı)* where Mehmet the Conqueror entered the fallen city in 1453. The double walls, built in the 5th century during the reign of Emperor Theodosius, stretch 6.5km (4 miles) from the Sea of Marmara to the Golden Horn. They were defended by 96 towers and had numerous gates. Much of the inner wall and several of the towers are still standing. Seven gates are still in use. It is possible to follow the walls as there are roads alongside them and in some places you can walk on the actual wall. The state of repair varies from section to section, and there is a great deal of painstaking renovation work being carried out.

The Adrianople Gate of the Theodosian Walls

Yedikule

At the Marmara end of the Theodosian Walls, far from the city's other sights but easily reached by bus or taxi, stands the ancient fortress of **Yedikule** (Seven Towers; open 9am–4.30pm; closed Wed; admission fee). It encloses the **Golden Gate** *(Altınkapı)*, the triumphal arch of the Byzantine emperors, which existed before the walls were built and was incorporated into them. In 1470 Mehmet the Conqueror further strengthened the ancient portal by building three towers of his own, linked by curtain walls to the four Byzantine towers flanking the Golden Gate. During Ottoman times the fortress was used as a prison and a treasury.

Eyüp and The Golden Horn (Haliç)

The **Golden Horn** is an inlet of the Bosphorus, penetrating 7.5km (4½ miles) into the hills behind the city. It forms a natural harbour, and in Ottoman times was the site of the Imperial Tershane (Naval Arsenal), capable of holding 120 ships. In later years it was an industrial area, but the factories and shipyards are now giving way to hotels and tourist attractions. Millions have also been spent on improving the water quality.

Aboard the ferry to Eyüp

Ferries depart from the upstream side of the Galata Bridge for the half-hour trip along the Golden Horn to the suburb of **Eyüp**, which contains one of Islam's most sacred shrines. The **Eyüp Sultan Camii** (mosque) marks the burial place of Eyüp Ensari, the standard-bearer of the Prophet Mohammed. He died in battle while carrying the banner of Islam during the Arab siege of Constantinople, between AD674 and 678.

Following the conquest in 1453, his grave was rediscovered, and Mehmet the Conqueror erected a shrine on the spot, followed in 1458 by a mosque, the first to be built in Istanbul. Thereafter each sultan, on his accession, visited Eyüp Camii to gird himself ceremonially with the Sword of Osman, the first Ottoman sultan. The original mosque was destroyed by an earthquake in 1766; the present building dates from 1800. The **Tomb of Eyüp Ensari**, behind the mosque, is decorated with gold, silver and coloured tiles, and is protected by a gilded grille. Remember that this is a sacred place – dress respectfully, remove your shoes before entering, and do not use a camera.

Covering the hillside behind the mosque is a vast cemetery littered with turbanned headstones. A path and cable car lead up to the **Pierre Loti Café**, named in honour of the 19th-century French writer who once lived in the neighbourhood, and who wrote romantic novels about life in Istanbul. The café enjoys a splendid view down the Golden Horn to the distant domes and minarets of Stamboul.

Pierre Loti

Louis Marie Julien Viaud (1859–1923) was a French naval officer whose travels took him to various places in the East and the South Seas. They provided a background for a steady stream of novels, about one per year, written under the pseudonym Pierre Loti. His books were once popular and highly regarded, but are now largely forgotten among English-speaking peoples.

Aziyadé, part autobiography and part romance, recounts his travels to Constantinople and his love affair with the green-eyed Circassian harem girl, Aziyadé. The book shows a passionate nature, and a man's dreams and melancholy in Constantinople in the last days of the Ottoman Empire. The café at Eyüp is where Pierre Loti is best remembered, though there's an eponymous restaurant and hotel in Sultanahmet.

St Stephen's church

On the south side of the Golden Horn, between the ferry stops of Fener and Balat, stands the Church of St Stephen of the Bulgars. This is a quite unique building, for the neo-Gothic structure and decorations are made entirely of iron. The sections were cast in Vienna and shipped down the Danube and across the Black Sea. It was built for Istanbul's Bulgarian community in 1871, and is still used in worship (currently closed for restoration).

On the north side of the Golden Horn, at Sutluce, is a children's favourite, **Miniaturk** (İmrahor Caddesi; open daily 9am–7pm; admission fee). Its miniature buildings (the scale is 25:1) have been selected to reflect the variety of civilisations found in and around Anatolia throughout history. A little further on, the **Rahmi M Koç Museum** (Hasköy Caddesi; open Tues–Fri 10am–5pm, Sat–Sun 10am–7pm; admission fee), housed in an old iron foundry on the south side of the Golden Horn, is a fascinating private collection of anything involving science, technology and transport, from an 1898 steam car to a 1940s American submarine as well as masses of smaller instruments, toys and hands-on things to play with. Perhaps not the obvious Turkish 'sight' but well worth visiting.

THE NEW CITY (BEYOĞLU)

The north shore of the Golden Horn was traditionally the quarter where craftsmen, foreign merchants and diplomats made their homes, beginning in the 11th century when the Genoese founded a trading colony in the district of Galata. Following the conquest, European ambassadors built their mansions on the hills beyond Galata, a place which came to be called Pera (Greek for 'beyond'). Foreigners from the entire Ottoman Empire flooded into Galata and

Pera, attracted by the wealth and sophistication of the capital. As the area became crowded, the wealthy foreign merchants and diplomats moved farther along the 'Grande Rue de Pera' (now İstiklal Caddesi), forming a focus for the 19th- and 20th-century expansion of the modern, European-style part of Istanbul, known as Beyoğlu.

Galata and Pera

The mouth of the Golden Horn is spanned by the **Galata Bridge**. The first bridge here was a wooden structure, built in 1845. It was replaced in 1910 by the famous old pontoon bridge with its seafood restaurants, which served until the present bridge was opened in 1992. Like the Atatürk Bridge farther upstream, its central span opens during the night to allow ships in and out. The bridge is thronged with fishermen and a waving forest of rods occupies every last piece of space. As you cross the Galata Bridge, your eyes are drawn naturally to the pointed turret of the Galata Tower. Sometime during the 11th century a rough bunch of coastal traders and drifters from every port in the Mediterranean began to settle on the northern shore of the Horn, in the maritime quarter which became known as Galata.

To avoid the steep climb up the hill beyond the Galata Bridge take the **Tünel**, the world's second oldest (and probably shortest) underground railway, built in 1875. The trip to the top station takes just 90 seconds *(see page 127)*. To reach the Galata Tower from the top station, follow the signs back down the hill.

Galata Tower

The **Galata Tower** (*Galata Kulesi*, open daily 9am–7pm; restaurant open till late) was the keystone in the colony's defences. Its age is uncertain, but it seems to have been built in its present form around 1349, at the highest point of the city walls. Now restored, with a restaurant at the top, it offers a fine view over the city, and across the Golden Horn you can count the minarets and domes of Old Istanbul's skyline.

At the top of the hill there are some shops selling books and musical instruments. There's also the **Galata Mevlevihanesi**, the former Whirling Dervish Hall, where Sufis whirled from 1491 until Atatürk proscribed their practices in 1924. The centre is now the Museum of Divan Literature, where manuscripts

Dervish graves

and a selection of instruments are preserved in glass cabinets, though there are still dervish performances held here (usually 3pm every second Sun in summer; notices of events are posted on the gates). The centre also provides a home for community of cats and kittens, who enjoy basking on the graves in the peaceful courtyard.

Just up the road, restored 1920s trams clang their way along **İstiklal Caddesi** (Avenue of Independence), once lined with the palatial embassies of foreign powers. The mansions have been downgraded to consulates since the capital was transferred to Ankara in 1923, and modern shops and restaurants have sprung up. The street is now pedestrianised, and has some of the city's smartest cafés. At Galatasaray Square, where İstiklal Caddesi bends to the right, an elegant wrought-iron gateway marks the entrance to the 19th-century **Galatasaray Lisesi**, the Franco-Turkish *lycée* (secondary school) that educated many of the great names in modern Turkish history. Just behind it is another of Istanbul's great historic hamams, the **Tarihi Galatasaray Hamamı** (Turnacıbaşı Sokak 24; open daily 7am–10pm for men, 8am–8pm for women).

Tram on İstiklal Caddesi

Past the square on the left is the entrance to **Çiçek Pasajı** (Flower Alley), a high, glass-roofed arcade lined with bars and restaurants. The opposite end of the arcade leads into the **Balık Pazarı** (Fish Market), a block of narrow streets lined with small restaurants and stalls selling fish, fruit and vegetables, and a local speciality snack – *midye tava* (fried mussels on a stick).

Turn left at Galatasaray Square, and left again at the British Consulate along Meşrutiyet Caddesi, and you will reach the **Pera Palas Hotel** (closed until late 2008 for renovation), established in 1892 to provide accommodation for Orient Express passengers. Agatha Christie stayed in Room 411 when writing *Murder on the Orient Express*. Room 101, the suite used by Atatürk, has been kept as a museum. Virtually opposite, the old Bristol Hotel is now the **Pera Museum** (Meşrutiyet Caddesi 141; open Tues–Sat 10am–7pm, Sun noon–6pm; admission fee), housing the Kiraç family collection of Kutahya

tiles, Anatolian weights and measures, and European portraits of life at the Ottoman imperial court. The top floor is used for temporary exhibitions of modern art.

Taksim and Beyond

Beyond Çiçek Pasajı, the side streets off İstiklal Caddesi are the focus for Istanbul's raunchier nightlife. The seedy bars, 'adult' cinemas, and nightclubs are best avoided, unless you want to spend all your money at once. But there are places with good music (from techno to jazz). The street ends at **Taksim Square** (*Taksim Meydanı*),

The Janissary Band in action

the heart of modern Istanbul, lined with hotels and the glass-fronted **Atatürk Cultural Centre** (*Atatürk Kültür Merkezi*; box office tel: (0212) 251 5600), with its array of theatres and concert halls. It is the main venue for the International Istanbul Festival.

At the far end of the square Cumhuriyet Caddesi leads past the Hilton Hotel for a good kilometre (³/₄ mile) to the **Military Museum** (*Askeri Müzesi*, open Wed–Sun 9am–5pm; admission fee includes the performance by the Janissary Band) in the northwestern corner of Yıldız Park. The exhibits include a section of the massive chain that the Byzantines used to stretch across the mouth of the Golden Horn to keep out enemy ships, as well as captured enemy cannon and military banners, the campaign tents from which the Ottoman sultans controlled their armies, and examples of uniforms, armour and weapons from the earliest days of the empire down to the 20th century. The main attraction is the concert given by the **Janissary Band** (*Mehter Takımı*), held daily between 3–4pm. The band is a revival of the Ottoman military band that accompanied the sultans' armies on campaigns and led the victory processions through the conquered cities. The colourful uniforms are exact replicas of the originals. Taksim Square also leads to the shopping districts of **Çukurcuma** – with its antiques dealers and cafés – and **Teşvikiye** and **Nişantaşı**, the Istanbul homes of designer labels.

The Bosphorus Shore

Karaköy Square, at the northern end of the Galata Bridge, is home to the local fish market and is a great place to begin a walk through the old docks area where the cruise-ship terminus is located. Housed in a former customs warehouse on Karaköy pier is **Istanbul Modern** (Meclis-I Mebusan Caddesi Liman Sahası; open Tues–Sun 10am–6pm, Thur 10am–8pm and free until 2pm; admission fee), which has a permanent collection of modern Turkish paintings, sculpture, photography, video and sound installations, as well as a room for touring exhibitions. There's also an art-house cinema and chic first floor café bar with superb views.

Dolmabahçe Palace

Take the tram along to the **Dolmabahçe Palace** (*Dolmabahçe Sarayı*; open Tues, Wed and Fri–Sun, Oct–Feb 9am–3pm, Mar–Sept 9am–4pm; admission fee, guided tours only). Sultan Abdül Mecit (reigned 1839–61), continuing the programme of reform begun by his father Mahmut II, decided that Topkapı Palace was too old-fashioned and commissioned a vast new palace on the shores of the Bosphorus, on the site of a park that had been created by filling in an old harbour *(dolmabahçe* means 'filled-in garden'). Completed in 1853, the palace was intended as a statement of the sultan's faith in the future of his empire, but instead it turned out to be a monument to folly and extravagance. Its construction nearly emptied the imperial treasury, and the running costs contributed to the empire's bankruptcy in 1875.

The guided tour is in two parts – first the **Selamlık** (public rooms) and **Throne Room**, then the **Harem** (private apartments). The highlights of the *Selamlık* include the vast Baccarat and Bohemian crystal chandeliers, 36 in all, and the crystal balusters of the main staircase, the sultan's bathroom, two huge bearskins (a gift from the Tsar of Russia), Sèvres vases, Gobelin tapestries and carpets, and the vast bed used by the 'giant sultan', Abdül Aziz. The Throne Room is huge and lavishly decorated.

At the north end of the park, the **Naval Museum** (Iskele Caddesi, Beşiktaş; open Wed–Sun 9am–5pm; admission fee) is a reminder that the Ottoman Empire was one of the world's great sea powers. This is a fascinating repository of naval memorabilia, from charts and the personal records,

The End of a Dynasty

It is appropriate that Dolmabahçe Palace, the main financial drain that contributed to the downfall of the empire in 1875, was witness to the final act of the empire.

When Atatürk's government abolished the sultanate in November 1922, Mehmet VI, the last representative of the dynasty that had ruled the Ottoman Empire for six centuries, was ignominiously smuggled aboard a British warship anchored off Dolmabahçe, to spend his last years in exile. Atatürk died in the palace on 10 November 1938 at 9.05am, the hour all the palace clocks were stopped.

clothes and belongings of Turkish sailors to the splendidly ornate Ottoman royal barges.

Just 2km (1½ miles) beyond Dolmabahçe you can escape from the city among the wooded walks of **Yıldız Palace and Park**. The ornate **Şale Köşkü** (Chalet Pavilion; open Tues–Sun 9.30am–4.30pm; admission fee) was built by Abdül Hamid II in 1882 for the sultan's guests, but the very paranoid Abdül Hamid moved in himself until he was deposed in 1909, living a solitary life as a carpenter roaming the lush gardens. Today it is a rather sad museum. Nearby **Malta Köşkü** is another restored royal pavilion that has been converted into a café, with a terrace looking over the treetops to the Bosphorus.

ACROSS TO ASIA

You can head from the hustle and bustle of Eminönü across the water to Asia. **Üsküdar** lies opposite, at the eastern shore of the Bosphorus. The ferry passes the **Kız Kulesi** (Maiden's Tower), perched on a tiny island about 200m offshore. The name is derived from a legend about a princess who was confined by her father to protect her from the fate foretold by a dire prophecy: that she would die from the bite of a serpent. Ironically, the princess was eventually bitten by a snake that arrived in one of the baskets containing supplies. Originally a 12th-century Byzantine fort, the present tower dates from the 18th century, and has served as a lighthouse, customs

The Maiden's Tower

office and control tower. It is now used as a restaurant and café with shuttle boat services from both sides of Istanbul. In Byzantine times a huge chain could be slung between here and the Saray Burnu Peninsula to close the mouth of the Bosphorus. The ferry leaves you at Üsküdar's main square, Iskele Meydanı. Note the **İskele Camii**, designed by Sinan in 1548 for Mihrimah, daughter of Süleyman the Magnificent, and the **Yeni Valide Camii** from the early 18th century. West of the square is Sinan's **Şemşi Paşa Camii** (1580).

Üsküdar is better known as Scutari by Europeans, and Scutari is traditionally associated with the name of Florence Nightingale. During the Crimean War (1854–6) the English nurse set up a hospital in what is now the enormous **Selimiye Barracks** (*Selimiye Kışlası*), situated in the district of Harem to the south of Üsküdar. A small corner of the building is kept as a **museum** in her memory – the exhibits include the famous lamp, which led to her being remembered under the affectionate title of 'The lady with the lamp' (for permission to visit fax (0216) 553 1009 two days ahead with your name, passport and contact details). Down a lane off Tibbiye Caddesi, the **Commonwealth War Graves Commission Haidar Pasha Cemetery** (*Commonwealth Harp Mezarligi Haidarpaşa*)

Commonwealth war graves

is a tranquil and beautiful spot. There is a huge memorial to the Crimean War, and the dead from the Crimea (mostly victims of cholera) and the two world wars rest in immaculate graves, with men from the UK and the Indian subcontinent lying side by side.

The Bosphorus ferry, with the Rumeli Hisarı and Fatih Sultan Mehmet Bridge in the background

LOCAL EXCURSIONS

Along the Bosphorus

The **Bosphorus** *(Istanbul Boğazı)* is the narrow strait linking the Black Sea to the Sea of Marmara, and separating the European part of Turkey from the vast hinterland of Anatolia. The winding channel is 30km (18 miles) long and about 2km (1½ miles) wide, narrowing to 750m (2,450ft) at Rumeli Hisarı.

The strait, once navigated by Jason and the Argonauts in their search for the Golden Fleece, and crossed on a bridge of boats by the Persian army of King Darius in 512BC en route to battle with the Scythians, is today busy with commercial shipping, ferries and fishing boats. Its wooded shores are lined with pretty fishing villages, old Ottoman mansions, and the villas of Istanbul's wealthier citizens. It is spanned by two impressive suspension bridges. The first bridge ever to link Europe and Asia was the **Bosphorus Bridge** (*Boğaziçi Köprüsü*) at Ortaköy, opened in 1973. It was followed in 1988 by the **Fatih Sultan Mehmet Bridge** at Rumeli Hisarı.

The **boat trip up the Bosphorus** (three sailings a day, 10.35am, noon and 1.35pm in summer) from the pier at Eminönü is worth every penny. The ferry weaves back and forth between Europe and Asia, calling first at Beşiktaş and then a string of attractive villages. You can remain on the boat for the round trip, or stop for lunch at Anadolu Kavağı, or disembark anywhere and return by bus or taxi. Plenty of private companies offer shorter cruises if you are pressed for time.

The ferry heads north, past the Istanbul Modern *(see page 59)* and the Çirağan Palace, now a luxury hotel, stopping at **Beşiktaş** where you can visit the Dolmabahçe Palace *(see page 59)*, the Naval Museum and Yıldız Park *(see page 61)*. From here you pass beneath the Bosphorus Bridge. Beneath its western end is **Ortaköy**, with its waterfront mosque. The village is a pleasant place, with shops, art galleries, bookstalls and cafés. Beyond the bridge, on the far shore, is the **Beylerbeyi Palace**, a sultan's summer residence and hunting lodge built in 1865 (guided tours Tues, Wed and Fri–Sun 9am–4pm, May–Sept until 5pm).

The sleek Bosphorus Bridge

If you continue past the rich suburbs of **Arnavutköy** and **Bebek**, famed for their wonderful *yalıs* (ornate wooden mansions on the waterfront), you will soon reach the massive fortress of **Rumeli Hisarı** (open daily except Wed 9am–4.30pm; admission fee). It was built at the command of Mehmet II in 1452 in preparation for his last assault on Constantinople. Its walls enclose a pleasant park with an open-air theatre that stages folk-dancing and concerts in summer. On the opposite shore is the smaller and older fortress of **Anadolu Hisarı** (closed to the public), dating from 1390. South of the fort is the ornate rococo façade of the **Küçüksu Pavilion** (open Tues–Wed and Fri–Sun 9.30am–4pm; admission fee), an Ottoman summer-house built on a favourite picnic spot known as the Sweet Waters of Asia.

Anadolu Kavağı

Beyond the Fatih Sultan Mehmet Bridge the boat stops at **Kanlıca** on the Asian shore, a village famous for its yoghurt, which you can sample at one of the waterside cafés. The upper reaches of the Bosphorus are lined with picturesque fishing villages – **Tarabya**, **Sarıyer** and **Rumeli Kavağı** – where you can enjoy a meal at one of the many seafood restaurants. In Sarıyer you can also visit the **Sadberk Hanım Museum** (open daily except Wed 10am–5pm; admission fee), a fabulous private collection covering the period from 500BC to Ottoman times, housed in two 19th-century villas. Well-presented displays of gold jewellery, embroidery, costumes and Anatolian figurines help make this one of the finest small museums in Turkey.

Last stop is **Anadolu Kavağı** on the Asian side, a picturesque place overlooked by a castle built by the Byzantines.

Bathers on Big Island

The ferry leaves you for a couple of hours or so. You will find a large choice of cafés in the village, and a fresh fish lunch is available.

The Princes' Islands

An hour's ferry-trip to the southwest of Istanbul lies the bucolic retreat of the **Princes' Islands**, known to the Turks simply as Adalar, 'The Islands'. This archipelago of nine islands in the Sea of Marmara has been inhabited ever since Byzantine times by monastic communities, and was used as a place of exile for deposed rulers. The Emperor Justin II built a palace on the largest island in the 6th century; it soon came to be known as Prinkipo, the Prince's Isle, and the name later spread to cover the whole group. Today the islands' pretty beaches provide the perfect weekend retreat location for the people of Istanbul. Cars are banned, and all transport is by foot, bicycle or horse-drawn carriage.

Check at the ferry terminal for times of ferries. Also check terminals for inter-island trips. The biggest and most popular island is **Büyükada** (Big Island), with a pleasant town and a picturesque monastery. You can take a tour of the island on a *fayton* (carriage) – to find the 'taxi rank', walk uphill from the jetty to the clock tower in the square and turn left. The tour will take you past **St George's Monastery**, where you can sample home-made wine as well as the healing waters of an *ayazma* (sacred spring). The iron rings in the marble floor of the chapel were used to restrain the mentally ill, who were once brought here hoping to be cured by the waters. The ferry also calls at the islands of **Kınalıada**, **Burgazada** and **Heybeliada**.

Belgrade Forest

This is an area north of Istanbul and west of Sarıyer. It was more or less a nature reserve kept for royal hunting. There was a village called Belgrade founded by Süleyman the Magnificent, who moved people from the other Belgrade into the area to look after reservoirs and aqueducts which provided Istanbul's water, so there are scattered remains of all this activity. Nowadays, people use the forest for picnics and exercise.

Black Sea

There are some small resorts accessible from Istanbul, pleasant and with sandy beaches and clean air. They can be reached by dolmuş or minibus. **Kilyos** on the European side is reached via Sarıyer. It is about 35km (22 miles) from the centre of Istanbul. The beach is long but the sea has some dangerous currents. The ruins of a Genoese castle can be seen but not visited as the area is in use by the military; however, there are some good walks. On the Asian side, there's transport from Üsküdar to **Şile**. It takes about an hour. Şile is fairly quiet during the week, but becomes the Brighton of Istanbul at the weekend. It has high cliffs and good fish restaurants.

OVERNIGHT EXCURSIONS

There are places of special interest that can be visited from Istanbul, but are sufficiently distant to require at least one overnight stop. They include the historic cities of Edirne, Bursa and İznik, and in winter there's a ski resort at Mount Uludağ, south of Bursa. However, many people want to visit Troy and Gallipoli. They usually stay overnight in **Çanakkale**, a seaside resort with hotels, restaurants and amenities, which also has a good Archaeological Museum.

Gallipoli

The **Gallipoli Peninsula** *(Gelibolu Yarımadası)*, on the north side of the Dardanelles, was the scene of one of the most notorious military campaigns of World War I. The Allied assault, involving Australian, British, New Zealand and

Anzac Cove at Gallipoli

French forces, aimed to capture the peninsula and control the narrow strait of the Dardanelles, thus securing an ice-free sea passage to supply arms to Russia and open a front against the Germans.

The first landings took place on 25 April 1915, and met with fierce resistance from the Turks, under the command of General Mustafa Kemal. The Allies only managed to gain a toehold on the peninsula, and then deadlock ensued, with almost nine months of static

'Our sons as well'

'There is no difference between the Johnnies and the Mehmets to us, where they lie side by side here in this country of ours. You, the mothers who sent their sons from faraway countries, wipe away your tears; Your sons are now lying in our bosom and are in peace after having lost their life on this land. They have become our sons as well.'

The words of Atatürk on a memorial at Gallipoli

trench warfare. The cost in human lives was terrible, with 160,000 Allies and 86,000 Turks dead and some 250,000 wounded. The Anzacs (Australia and New Zealand Army Corps) saw some of the worst fighting and suffered the heaviest casualties; the beach where they landed has been named **Anzac Cove** *(Anzak Köyü)* in their honour.

The whole peninsula is a memorial, with plaques describing the campaign's progress, and monuments to the soldiers of the Allied and Turkish armies. Begin at one of the two museums, at the Çamburnu Park Headquarters, 1km (½ mile) from the ferry at Eceabat, or the Kabatepe Military Museum (both open daily 8.30am–5.30pm; closed lunchtime in winter; admission fee). Each war cemetery is signposted, and all are beautifully tended, planted with flowers and scented with fragrant hedges of rosemary. A memorial service attended by families of Turkish and Anzac veterans as well as other visitors is held each year on Anzac Day (25 April).

Troy

The exact location of the legendary city of Troy (open daily 8.30am–5pm; admission fee) remained a mystery until an amateur archaeologist with a passion for Homer began excavations in 1871. Heinrich Schliemann found his fabled city, and discovered 'Priam's treasure', a cache of gold. He smuggled it back to Germany, but it vanished during World War II, only to make a dramatic reappearance in Moscow in 1993.

Archaeologists have now uncovered nine superimposed cities, from Troy I, an Early Bronze Age settlement (3000–2500BC) to the Hellenistic and Roman metropolis, known as Ilium Novum, which stood here from 334BC to AD400. American scholars identify the level known as Troy VIIa as King Priam's city, and place its destruction around 1260BC. Certain eminent Turkish archaeologists disagree, instead opting for the preceding level, Troy VI.

The site, near the village of **Hısarlık**, is marked by a large replica of the famed wooden horse. For those who have enjoyed Homer's *Iliad* and *Odyssey* it is a magical place, where the stones are haunted by the spirits of Helen and Paris, Achilles and Agamemnon.

The Trojan Horse

Most people know the story of the Trojan War as Homer told it. It all started when peace-loving King Priam's son, Paris, was inveigled by a trio of jealous goddesses into abducting the most beautiful woman in the world, Helen, wife of Menelaus, king of Sparta.

The ensuing war between Greece and Troy lasted 10 years and cost the lives of great heroes such as Hector and Achilles. The end came when the Greeks tricked the Trojans into accepting a gift of a huge wooden horse within their walls – it was filled with armed men who sacked the city and left it in ruins.

The Aegean coastline

AEGEAN COAST

Turkey's Aegean coast offers an unparalleled combination of natural beauty and historical interest. This was one of the most densely populated parts of the ancient world, with many famous cities to its name – Troy, city of the *Iliad* and the *Odyssey,* and Smyrna (İzmir), the birthplace of Homer; Sardis, home of the wealthy King Croesus; Ephesus, where St Paul preached the gospels; and Halicarnassos, birthplace of the historian Herodotus. The ruins of two of the Seven Wonders of the World – the Temple of Artemis at Ephesus and the Mausoleum of Halicarnassus – are also to be found here.

Set amid these historic sites are many beautiful beaches and pretty fishing villages, and a number of modern holiday resorts, notably Kuşadası and Bodrum. The main city is İzmir, which has an international airport; there are other airports at Bodrum and Dalaman, where most package tours arrive.

İzmir and the Northern Aegean

Known to the Greeks as Smyrna, and to the Turks as '*Güzel İzmir*' (Beautiful İzmir), Turkey's third-largest city sprawls around the head of the finest natural harbour on the Aegean coast. **İzmir** was founded in the 3rd millennium BC on the north shore of the bay, and reached a peak during the 10th century BC, when it was one of the most important cities in the Ionian Federation – the poet Homer was born in Smyrna during this period. After the Lydian conquest of the 6th century BC the city lost its importance, but was refounded by Alexander the Great on the slopes of Mount Pagus (now Kadifekale). Under the Greeks and Romans it became one of the principal centres of Mediterranean trade.

When the Ottoman Turks took control in the 15th century, İzmir grew wealthy as a merchant city, handling Smyrna figs and Turkish tobacco from the farms of the interior, and allowing the establishment of European trading colonies. It prospered as a port until the close of the Greco-Turkish War in 1922, when it was almost completely destroyed by bitter fighting and fire. Rebuilt around the site of Alexander's city, it is once again a bustling port and industrial city, the third largest in Turkey, but almost no trace remains of its former glory.

The heart of the city is **Konak Meydanı**, a square distinguished by two famous monuments. The **Saat Kulesi** (Clock Tower), dating from 1901, is the unofficial symbol of İzmir. Nearby stands the

King Aegeus

The Aegean is called after King Aegeus, whose adopted son, Theseus, went off to kill the Minotaur. Theseus was helped by Ariadne, who loved him. He deserted her and so taken up was he with his adventures, he forgot a promise to change the black mourning sail from his ship for a white one – and as his ship sailed home, Aegeus thought that Theseus was dead and threw himself to his death in the water.

tiny **Konak Camii** (mosque), built in 1756 and decorated with colourful Kütahya tile panels. On the hill to the south of the square stands the **Archaeological Museum** (open daily 8.30am–noon 1–5pm, to 6pm in summer; admission fee), whose superb collection of antiquities includes statues of Poseidon and Demeter that once stood in the Agora of ancient Smyrna.

Tiles in the Konak Mosque

The nearby Ethnographic Museum (*Etnografya Muzesi*; open Tues–Sun 8.30am–noon and 1–5pm, 5.30pm in summer) recreates such treats as the interiors of traditional local houses, an Ottoman pharmacy, a bridal chamber, a circumcision room and exhibits on the manufacture of the 'evil eye' amulets and camel wrestling. Inland from the Konak Mosque is İzmir's **bazaar**, one of the best in Turkey.

North of Konak Meydanı, **Atatürk Caddesi** (also known as the **Kordon**) runs along the waterfront to the ferry port at Alsancak, 3km (2 miles) away. A horse-drawn phaeton will take you on a tour, which passes through **Cumhuriyet Meydanı** (Republic Square), the centre of modern İzmir, surrounded by glittering luxury hotels and palm-fringed promenades. Nearby is the **Kültür Parkı**, a huge, shady pleasure garden, venue of the annual International Fair. Uphill, through the huge bazaar, lies the **Agora** (open daily 8.30am–noon, 1–5pm; admission fee), one of the few remaining traces of İzmir's ancient history. This colonnaded square, built during the 2nd century AD, was once the city's bustling marketplace. At the top of the hill is the imposing medieval fortress of **Kadifekale**. This was the

Legacy of slavery

İzmir has a black community – Turkish-speaking descendants of slaves from the Sudan, who were brought to Turkey in the 16th to 19th centuries.

ancient Mount Pagus, where Alexander the Great commanded his generals Lysimachus and Antigonus to found a new city back in the 4th century BC. However, no trace remains of their original fortifications.

Pergamon

The modern city of Bergama is 171km (107 miles) north of İzmir. The ruins of **Pergamon** tower nearby. The Bergama Archaeological Museum (open daily 8.30am–noon, 1–5pm; admission fee) is in the centre of the modern town. It has a large collection of material from Stone Age to Byzantine times.

At the height of its power, in the 2nd century BC, Pergamon (open daily, 8.30am–7pm in summer, to 5.30pm in winter; admission fee) was one of the most splendid cities on the Aegean coast. Its acropolis was capped with magnificent buildings, and it had a library of over 200,000 volumes (the Pergamenes are credited with the invention of parchment). Its ruins, high above the modern town of Bergama, are still impressive.

The **acropolis** was built on a set of terraces. On the left of the entrance ramp is the open space once occupied by the **Temple of Athena**, close to which are the remains of the **Pergamene library**. Its contents were eventually given to the beautiful Cleopatra as a gift from Mark Antony, and went to enrich the famous library of Alexandria.

Beyond the library is the city's most splendid building, its glittering white marble columns, now partly restored. The **Trajaneum** was erected during the 2nd century AD in honour of the deified emperors Trajan and Hadrian.

Below the Temple of Athena is the steep *cavea* of the **theatre**, set in a shallow depression in the hillside. Nearby is the base of the **Altar of Zeus**, built to commemorate the defeat of the Gauls by the Romans in 190BC. This was once decorated with a remarkable frieze depicting the Battle of the Gods and Giants, one of the finest existing examples of Hellenistic sculpture, which now resides in Berlin's Pergamon Museum.

Visible on the plain below is the **Asclepion**, one of the ancient world's leading medical centres, rivalling similar establishments at Epidauros, Kos and Ephesus. Dedicated to Asclepius, god of healing, the Asclepion provided hot baths, massages, dream interpretation, primitive psychiatry, and draughts of water from a sacred spring (found to be mildly radioactive). Galen (AD130– 200), the most famous physician in the ancient world after Hippocrates, practised here.

The entrance to the Asclepion is located along a colonnaded street, the Sacred Way, which leads to the **medical precinct**. Here you can see the remains of the library, theatre and treatment rooms. In the middle of the square is a pool fed by the sacred spring.

Trajaneum at Pergamon

Sardis

The site of Sardis (open daily 8am–6pm in summer; 8am–1pm, 2–5pm in winter, but access easy at other times; admission fee) is usually visited from İzmir, though the nearest accommodation is Salihili which is just 9km (6 miles)

Scenery near Sardis

away. Sardis, the former capital of ancient Lydia, is 100km (60 miles) east of İzmir, on the road to Uşak and Afyon.

Sardis was once the wealthiest city in the world, under the famous King Croesus (reigned 560–546BC), hence the expression 'rich as Croesus.' During his reign, the Lydians invented coinage, producing the first-ever coins of gold and silver, stamped with the royal emblem: a lion's head. The gold was washed down from the hills by the River Pactolus; the Greek historian Herodotus relates how flakes of the precious metal were trapped in the fleece of sheepskins spread in the stream-bed, perhaps giving rise to the legend of the Golden Fleece.

Intent on expanding his empire into Persian-held territory, Croesus consulted the oracle at Delphi. It told him that if he attacked the Persians he would destroy a great empire. He attacked anyway, and was crushed – the empire he destroyed was his own. The monuments you see today date from Roman and Byzantine times.

The principal ruins of Sardis are in two parts. On the left side of the main highway you will find the **Gymnasium complex**. From the car park you follow a line of **ancient shops** to a gate at the far end, which leads into the **synagogue**, whose floor is richly decorated with mosaic patterns. The gymnasium itself, a huge open square, is dominated by the magnificently restored **Marble Court**, lined with ornate marble columns and niches which once held statues. The arched gateway leads to a large swimming pool and the ruins of a Roman and Byzantine **baths** complex.

In the nearby village, a side road leads south for 1km (½ mile) to the imposing **Temple of Artemis** (separate admission) begun during the reign of Alexander the Great, and abandoned, unfinished, following the ascendancy of Christianity in the 4th century. The enormous structure had a peristyle of 52 columns, of which two still stand at their full height. A small 5th-century Byzantine church hides behind the columns at the far end.

Çeşme

A six-lane toll motorway leads 80km (50 miles) west of İzmir to the small resort and ferry port of Çeşme, where boats cross daily to the Greek island of Chios, a mere 12km (7½ miles) away. The town was a quiet spa and beach resort (its name means 'drinking fountain') until the motorway's arrival brought it within comfortable commuting distance of the city; now it is set to become a bustling seaside suburb of İzmir, and a terminal for international ferries from Italy and Greece.

The town is dominated by an Ottoman **fortress** built in the 16th century (open daily 8.30am–7.30pm; admission fee). Beside the fortress lies an 18th-century **caravanserai**, or inn, which has been converted into a hotel, and now hosts regular 'folklore evenings' of Turkish dance and music. On the main shopping street, amongst the many carpet and jewellery shops, you will find an attractive and interesting art gallery housed in the ancient Greek basilica of Ayios Haralambos.

There are a few other sights to see – the main attractions are the golden-sand **beaches** at **Ilıca**, home to several **hot springs**. The warm, sulphurous waters (around 35–50°C/95–122°F) are said to be good for rheumatism and respiratory complaints.

Kuşadası and Environs

Situated on a small promontory, **Kuşadası**, meaning 'Island of Birds', is one of Turkey's liveliest and most popular holiday resorts. The town, 80km (50 miles) south of İzmir, has a large yachting marina, and serves as a port for Mediterranean cruise ships. Attractions here include some pleasant beaches, a vibrant nightlife and the nearby ruins of Ephesus.

White-washed houses climb the hill above the harbour, where ferries depart daily for the Greek island of Samos, and

Kuşadası

lively bars and restaurants line the streets of the old quarter. The busy **bazaar** clusters around the walls of a 17th-century *caravanserai,* now converted into a hotel; across the street, seafood restaurants skirt the quay of the old harbour.

Beyond the modern ferry port, a 350-m (1,050-ft) causeway connects Kuşadası to **Güvercin Adası** (Pigeon Island), which is topped by a 13th-century Byzantine castle and ringed with gardens and colourful cafés.

A dolmuş service links the town to Ladies' Beach *(Kadınlar Plajı),* 3km (2 miles) to the south, and there are also beaches at **Pamucak** and in the **Dilek National Park** *(Dilek Yarımadası Milli Parkı),* 25km (15½ miles) from town.

Efes (Ephesus)

Ephesus is 17km (10½ miles) inland from Kuşadası, and is usually visited on a trip from there, though the closest town is **Selçuk**, a small town 19km (12 miles) northeast of Kuşadası. Selçuk has taxis, restaurants, hotels and some lively bars, and the **Selçuk Museum** (open Tues–Sun 8.30am–noon and 1–5pm, to 7pm in summer; admission fee) has an exceptional archaeological section, including the famous 'many breasted Artemis'; and a fine ethnographical section. There are also several noteworthy monuments in and around town, including the 6th-century **Basilica of St John**, on Ayasuluk Hill, which supposedly marks the site of the Apostle's tomb. The fortress above dates from Byzantine times. Downhill you will find the impressive **Isa Bey Mosque** (1375), and beyond is a solitary column marking the site of the once-great **Temple of Artemis**.

Ephesus itself is one of the best-preserved and most visited of Turkey's ancient cities (open summer 8am–6.30pm, to 5.30pm in winter; admission fee). Its marble streets and monuments have been extensively excavated and restored by archaeologists, and with only a little imagination it is easy to transport yourself to Roman times.

Ionian Greeks from the island of Samos settled in Ephesus around 1000BC. The site was associated with the worship of the Anatolian mother-goddess Cybele, who became merged with the Greek Artemis. The great Temple of Artemis, one of the Seven Wonders of the World, was erected in her honour. The city was ruled in turn by the Lydians, the Persians and the Attalid kings of Pergamon, until 133BC, when Attalus III bequeathed his kingdom, and Ephesus with it, to the Romans. Ephesus was one of the most important cities in the new province of Asia, with a population of 200,000, and grew wealthy on the proceeds of trade. But its greatness was linked to its fine harbour, and when this silted up in the 3rd century AD, the city went into decline. The site was rediscovered by the British archaeologist JT Wood in 1869 after six years of searching. Many of the ruins that you see today date from the Roman period, between the 1st century BC and 2nd century AD.

Most guided tours begin at the **Magnesian Gate** and head downhill along the main street. The first buildings inside the gate are the well-preserved **Odeum** (council chamber), with its semi-circular seats, and the **Prytaneum**, where archaeologists found the two statues of Artemis, now on display in the

Mary's House

Legend has it that St John the Apostle brought the Virgin Mary to Ephesus around AD37–48. Situated in the Bulbul Hills just south of Ephesus, the Meryemana (Mary's House) is where she is thought to have passed the last years of her life. It was discovered during the 19th century by priests from İzmir following instructions given by a German nun, Anna Katharina Emmerich, who had seen it in a vision. There is now a chapel occupying the site, which has long been a place of pilgrimage, but the building's foundations may date from the 1st century. Whether you're religious or not, it's a lovely walk into the pine-scented hills.

The Library of Celsus at Ephesus

Selçuk Museum. The marble-paved **Street of the Curetes**, its stone rutted by ancient cart wheels, leads through the Gate of Hercules to the remarkable **Temple of Hadrian**, with an arched doorway capped by the head of Tyche, goddess of fortune. At the corner of Marble Street, on the right, are the **Baths of Scholastica**, which also included a brothel.

Rising up ahead is the imposing façade of the **Library of Celsus**, built in AD110 by a Roman consul as a memorial to his father. Beautiful statues of the four virtues – Episteme (Knowledge), Sophia (Wisdom), Ennoia (Thought) and Arete (Valour) – adorn the niches between the columns.

Marble Street leads from the library to the **Great Theatre**, the probable setting for the riot of the silversmiths described in the Bible (Acts 19:24–41). Its vast *cavea* provided seating for 25,000 people, and still accommodates the crowds who gather for performances during the annual International Festival of Arts and Culture *(see page 98)*. From the top rows of seats you can enjoy a grand view of the Arcadian Way, the city's colonnaded main street, once lined with fine statues, and lit by oil lamps at night. At its far end a scrub-filled depression marks the site of the former harbour, long since silted up.

Pamukkale and Hierapolis

One popular excursion from the Aegean resorts is to the spectacular travertine terraces of **Pamukkale** (the Cotton Castle; open daily sunrise–sunset; admission fee), above the town of **Denizli**, about 200km (125 miles) inland from Kuşadası.

This remarkable natural formation has been created by mineral-rich hot springs cascading down the hillside and depositing layers of calcium carbonate. The resulting pools, terraces and 'petrified waterfalls' of dazzling white travertine are one of Turkey's most famous sights. The ruins of ancient **Hierapolis** lie scattered on the hillside behind the

Petrified waterfalls at Pamukkale

terraces, adding historical interest to natural beauty. The **Antique Pool** is a therapeutic, restorative spring whose waters will float you above a picturesque jumble of broken columns and Corinthian capitals.

A trip to Pamukkale also usually includes a visit to the site of the ancient city of **Aphrodisias** (open daily, summer 8am–7pm; winter to 5.30; admission fee). The city, dedicated to the worship of Aphrodite, goddess of love, was famous for its superb sculpture. The ruins, which are still being excavated, include one of the best-preserved stadia in Turkey, 228m (748ft) long, with seating for 30,000, and the remarkable Sebasteion, a porticoed gallery of sculpture dedicated to Aphrodite and the Roman Emperor.

The hotels are all in the village of Karahayıt, on the plateau nearby, which has multi-coloured travertines, hot springs and spas and excellent, ridiculously cheap cotton clothing.

South of Kuşadası

Between Selçuk and Bodrum lie three important archaeological sites that can all be easily seen in one day.

Priene (open 8.30am–sunset; admission fee), once one of the most active ports in the Ionian Federation, now stands about 5km (3 miles) inland, due to the silting up of the River Maeander. It enjoys a beautiful location on a higher terrace overlooking the plain, backed by the steep crag of the acropolis. The theatre, *bouleterion* (council chamber) and agora are worth exploring, but the main attraction is the great **Temple of Athena**. Alexander the Great, who passed through the city in 334BC, paid for its completion; five of the original 30 columns have been restored to their full height.

The silt of the River Maeander has also stranded the once-mighty city of **Miletus** (open daily 8am–5pm; admission fee). Its harbour, from which Milesian ships set forth to found over 100 colonies during the 7th and 8th centuries BC, is now a frog-filled marsh. Some idea of its former glory can be gleaned from the ruins of the agora, theatre and the Baths of Faustina.

No city ever stood at **Didyma**, just the colossal **Temple of Apollo**, one of the largest and most elegant temples in the ancient world. Only two columns still stand, but the forest of massive marble stumps gives some idea of the grandeur of the original building. People would travel great distances to consult the oracle of Apollo, seeking advice on business issues, marriage and military campaigns. When the Persians destroyed Miletus in 494BC, they also razed the Temple of Apollo at Didyma. Its reconstruction was begun by Alexander the Great (his victory over the Persians at Gaugamela in 331BC was predicted by the oracle), and continued for centuries, but the temple was never completed – some of the columns remain unfluted.

Bodrum

The picture-postcard resort of Bodrum occupies the site of ancient Halicarnassos, famed as the city of King Mausolus, whose tomb was one of the Seven Wonders of the World, as well as the birthplace of Herodotus, the 'Father of History'. Little remains of Halicarnassos, however, and the town's main attractions include its laid-back, Bohemian atmosphere, a beautiful double bay backed by whitewashed houses, and the magnificent **Crusader Castle** that dominates the harbour. No wonder it has been dubbed the St Tropez of Turkey. The attractions of Bodrum, however, have not

Beaches and hotels

There are no good beaches in Bodrum itself, but you have the choice of taking a boat trip from the harbour to one of the many coves that lie along the coast of the peninsula to the west. Most of the hotels that claim to be in Bodrum are actually in one of the many heavily developed villages on this peninsula, including Turgutreis, Gümüşlük, Yalıkavak and Türkbükü.

gone unnoticed – it gets very crowded here during the summer months.

The **Castle of St Peter** (open Tues–Sun 9am–noon, 2–7pm, check times as different sections open at different times; admission fee) was built in the 15th century by the Knights of St John, who used stone quarried from the ruins of the Mausoleum of Halicarnassos. It fell to the Ottomans in 1523, and its various buildings now house a fine collection of antiquities, including a fascinating **Museum of Underwater Archaeology**. Among the highlights are the medieval Glass Wreck, the Kas-Uluburun Shipwreck,

Boats in Bodrum

the Late Roman Shipwreck and the Hall of the Carian Princess with a royal tomb from about 360BC. The **towers** offer splendid views across the town and harbour. In the **English Tower** the banqueting hall has been restored, and you can read the graffiti carved in the window niches by homesick knights.

The site of the **Mausoleum**, the tomb of King Mausolus, is set a few blocks in from the harbour. It was begun around 355BC at the behest of the king (the word 'mausoleum' is derived from his name) and remained standing until at least the 12th century. By the time the Crusaders arrived in 1402 it was in ruins, destroyed by an earthquake. Today, nothing remains except the foundations. An exhibition hall displays several versions as to how the building may have looked.

WHAT TO DO

SHOPPING

Istanbul's markets and bazaars offer some of the world's most interesting – and challenging – opportunities for shopping. A huge variety of handmade goods finds its way into the city from towns and villages all over Turkey, much of it of very high quality – wool and silk carpets, kilims (flat-weave rugs), *cicims* (embroidered kilims), leather goods, ceramics and pottery, copper and brassware, and jewellery.

The principal shopping area in Istanbul is the Grand Bazaar, with more than 4,000 shops crammed beneath its roof. Running downhill from here is Uzunçarşı Caddesi, lined with hardware shops, which leads to the Spice Bazaar, the best place to buy *lokum* (Turkish Delight). The weekend flea market in Beyazıt Square is an interesting place to browse, and there are bargains to be found. Across from the square are the backstreets of Laleli, the place to look for low-priced clothes. Shopping isn't confined to the market. For more modern upmarket shopping, try the stylish boutiques of Nişantaşı and Teşvikiye, near Taksim Square, or head west to the Galleria shopping mall by the marina at Ataköy or east to the Kanyon Mall in Levent. There are also plenty of smart shops along İstiklal Caddesi. For craft shops, antique dealers and galleries, try Çukurcuma in Galatasaray, or Ortaköy on a Saturday or Sunday. For leather go to Zeytinbürnu, halfway to the airport.

Bargaining
Handmade items each have a different value, depending on the quality of the craftsmanship it shows; bargaining is a way

Lokum (Turkish Delight) at the Spice Market

No two carpets are identical

of determining an appropriate price. It isn't a way for a shopkeeper to get money out of a customer. If you want to buy something, shop around and find out how much shopkeepers ask and then offer about half of what you are prepared to pay. The owner will feign amazement at your insultingly low offer and you'll plead poverty. Furthermore, you add, you can get it cheaper elsewhere. Good-natured banter continues until you reach a mutually acceptable price. Large purchases can take time, several glasses of tea and a good half-hour of discussion. Remember: never begin bargaining for something you don't intend to buy, and never quote a price you are not prepared to pay.

In resorts, traders are often aware that tourists are uncomfortable bargaining and so they simply offer a 'best price' if that's what you ask. This is the least they'll be able to accept and there's no point discussing anything as their profit margins are slender. Sometimes, items on sale in the resorts and areas frequented by tourists are not of the best quality.

What to Buy

You need an export licence to take a genuine antique out of the country, and this involves getting a certificate. If you buy an old-looking item, even if it's clearly fake, get a *fatura*, an invoice from the dealer stating the piece's value and when and where it was made, because the customs people may need convincing. A reputable dealer will organise a certificate for you.

Carpets and kilims. No two carpets are identical. Patterns and symbols are handed down and have significance, conferring good luck and protection from the evil eye.

Carpet prices reflect the age, rarity, quality of materials and dyes, and tightness of weave. The number of knots in a square centimetre ranges from 20–30 for a coarse wool carpet to 100–200 in a silk carpet. The amount of work is reflected in the price. Natural dyes cost more than synthetic ones. It is worth doing your homework, and asking a few pertinent questions will make the seller less likely to fob you off with an inferior item. Kilims are rugs which are woven, rather than knotted. A *cicim* is a kilim with embroidered decoration.

Ceramics and pottery. The kilns at İznik near Bursa produced the best ceramic tiles ever, and these are now collector's items. You'll have to make do with polychrome tiles, bowls and vases, some of which copy the traditional designs but are affordable.

Copper and brass. Glittering, hand-beaten pieces are available in the shops of the Old Bedesten in the Grand Bazaar and on Bakircilar Caddesi, behind Beyazıt Square Braziers, shoeshine boxes, lamps, candlesticks, coffee grinders and samovars are ready to buy. Coppersmiths will be happy to make items to order or engrave a purchase.

Copper and brassware

Leather and suede. Handbags, wallets, belts, jackets, trousers, coats and skirts are all bargains. The leather is generally good quality but sometimes the stitching is poor, so check on the workmanship before you commit yourself. Clothing and shoes can be made to order, but bear in mind that good-quality work takes time.

Jewellery. The best place to look for quality jewellery is Old Bedesten in the Grand Bazaar. Some cheaper items can be found in Kalpakcilar Basi Caddesi (the main street of the bazaar). Gold is sold by weight, and prices are posted daily in the bazaar. There's a surcharge for workmanship. Genuine sterling silver is hallmarked. There are many cheap imitations on the market with fake stones and silver plating, so beware of rip-offs, especially in shops in resorts.

Clothing. Turkey is one of the world's largest suppliers of cotton and cotton clothing, including many big name brands. Good quality cotton clothing is excellent value, while the resorts often have great designer boutiques.

Other items. In the resorts sponges of all shapes and sizes can be found. A speciality of Bodrum is hand-crafted leather sandals. You might consider buying a hubble-bubble pipe, a nargile, the kind smoked by old men in Turkish cafés, or a highly decorated chess or backgammon board. There are beautiful meerschaum pipes and figurines, too.

You can't leave without a *nazar boncuk*, the evil-eye amulet. Remember, if ever you find it cracked, it's done its job and you need a replacement. Prayerbeads, musical instruments and puppets also make good souvenirs.

Books

When it comes to learning about Turkey, few bookshops can match the offerings of Galeri Kayseri at Divanyolu 58, in the heart of Sultanahmet. It holds a staggering collection of books on topics ranging from architecture and art to handicrafts, history, Sufism and Islam.

The Book Market (Sahasar Çarsısı) by the Grand Bazaar

ENTERTAINMENT

Nightlife

Nightlife is a feature of the Aegean resorts – bars pump out music, live or otherwise, with Turkish or English lyrics. There is probably something for everyone among the ubiquitous English and Irish pubs and other bars, and the entertainments. Turkish evenings and other treats are available.

In Istanbul, nightlife is to be found on Istiklal Caddesi and the surrounding streets, around the Taksim area and along the European shore of the Bosphorus. There isn't much revelry in the old city, so if you prefer a quiet supper and early bed, that's the place for you. Of course, there are rip-off joints, where you will be charged an astronomical amount, and forcibly relieved of your wallet if you don't pay up, but these are outnumbered by places which are good value.

Turkish-style supper clubs called *gazinos* offer an evening of folk music and belly dancing, often with dinner and drinks included. Most package tours offer an evening as part of the deal. Otherwise hotels and travel agents can make arrangements. It isn't difficult to find a *gazino* anyway. There are cabarets for those who like to dress up and pay up. And some of them are worth it. Top-class belly dancers are astonishing.

Istanbul has a thriving club scene, and there are clubs to suit various tastes with DJs, live bands, booze and babes. Aside from Turkish pop *(see opposite)*, everything from jazz and rock to house and hip-hop is on offer, in some club or other. Turkey is somewhat ambivalent about gay life, but there are gay clubs. However, as in the West, there is an immense enthusiasm for transvestite and transsexual singers and entertainers in Turkey, and there are assorted transvestite bars and shows.

Bars and Pubs

Although Islamic, Turkey is far from 'dry'. Istanbul has plenty of places where you may raise the wrist: the James Joyce Pub, Harry's Jazz Bar (in the Hyatt Regency), Hayal Kahvesi (bar/café with live Turkish music in Beyoğlu) and many others. There are also good bars in Ataköy (southwest of the

Belly Dancing

This ancient art is thought to have its origins in Africa. It is a popular entertainment for locals as well as tourists, and the best dancers are famous, often appearing on TV.

A belly dance is not just a performance, it's an invitation to join in – any Turkish gent worth his salt will be up shimmying on the dance floor at the earliest opportunity. Even if you don't join in, you can show your appreciation by moistening a bank-note and sticking it on the dancer's forehead, or – despite principles of equality – tucking it into her bra or waistband.

city), and in Ortaköy and Bebek on the Bosphorus. In recent years a growing number of very chic venues have opened, such as 360° and Vogue, which start the evening as cocktail lounges, continue as restaurants and end the night as dance clubs for the beautiful people.

Pop Music

Turkey has developed its own exuberant pop scene, with influences coming from folk rhythms, traditional tunes, the tango (which was at one time popular) and Arab and Western pop music. Well-known Turkish pop stars are Mustafa San-

Belly dancer in action

dal, Nilufer and Sezen Aksu. Turkey is enthusiastic about the Eurovision song contest, and Sertab Erener was a popular winner in 2003 with *Every Way That I Can*. Tarkan is Turkey's superstar, having a fan base outside the country. His hit *Simarik* was covered in English by Holly Valance as *Kiss Kiss*.

Sound and Light Show

From June to September you can enjoy a free sound-and-light show at the Blue Mosque (the viewing benches are about halfway between the mosque and Aya Sofya). The show, which begins each evening at 9pm, relates in melodramatic fashion the history of Istanbul, while coloured floodlights illuminate the spectacular architecture of the Blue Mosque.

The commentary is in English, French, German or Turkish, in rotation – check the notice by the benches for the time of the next performance in English.

Classical Music and Cinema

The Atatürk Cultural Centre on Taksim Square offers a programme of opera, ballet and symphony concerts from October to May; during the Istanbul International Festival, held from mid-June to mid-July, the city hosts musicians and performers from all over the world. Jazz is popular in Istanbul, and many bars and clubs have live bands performing on weekends.

There are many cinemas on İstiklal Caddesi, which show mainstream movies. Look for the word 'orijinal' on the poster – this means that the film will be shown in its original language, with Turkish subtitles; otherwise it has been dubbed.

SPORTS

Spectator Sports

Football is Turkey's favourite sport and there are three internationally famous Istanbul teams: Galatasaray, Fenerbahçe and Beşiktaş. Some provincial teams are to be respected also. To admire Turkish football is one way to make friends.

Matches are played in Istanbul, and whether they're Turkish league or European games, the atmosphere is always electric. The British media in particular has given much coverage to the perceived hostility of Turkish fans; however, encounters between both teams and fans are usually good-natured.

Unique to Turkey is the national sport of oiled wrestling (*yağlı güreş*). An annual gathering is held in June at Kırkpınar, near Edirne, 230km (143 miles) northwest of Istanbul. The competitors, wearing only a pair of leather breeches, coat themselves in olive oil and perform a ceremonial procession before getting to grips with their slippery opponents and flinging each other around, to the delighted cheers of thousands of spectators.

An even more exotic spectacle is camel wrestling *(deve güreşi)*, which can be seen only in January (the camels' breeding season) at Selçuk, near Kuşadası. These hump-backed beasts are bad-tempered, and when two moody males confront each other in the ring, a fierce sparring match ensues, in which they use their necks to try to throw each other off balance. Before they get injured they are separated, and the winner is decided by a panel of judges while the loser is dragged off.

A choice of teams to support

Horse racing may seem rather tame by comparison. Races are held between April and December at the Veliefendi Hippodrome near Bakırköy, 15km (9 miles) west of Istanbul. In winter, they move to İzmir.

In 2005, Turkey held its first Formula 1 Grand Prix at Tuzla, just outside Istanbul, on the Asian shore.

Active Pursuits
The Turkish government encourages the development of sport and leisure activities, so new facilities are being opened. There are a couple of long-established golf courses in Istanbul. Tennis, basketball and volleyball and other sports and games are often offered in the Aegean resorts.

Polluted water around Istanbul means that one needs to go to one of the beaches outside the city. The best beaches within easy reach are the Black Sea resorts. There are good swimming beaches on the Princes' Islands, too, but they get extremely crowded at weekends. West of the city, there are beaches at Florya (20km/12½ miles), and farther out at Silivri and Gümüşyaka (65km/40 miles).

Water sports. The Aegean really comes into its own with water sports, including assorted forms of sailing, windsurfing, kitesurfing, scuba diving, snorkelling, paragliding, water-skiing, canoeing, banana-boat rides, jet skiing and more!

Paragliding at the coast

The resorts have instructors and schools for most activities, teaching beginners, bubble blowers and advanced courses. These are strictly controlled by the authorities and the instructors have recognised qualifications. There are diving excursions for competent divers, like visiting underwater wrecks or archaeological sites. If you're not keen on getting wet, you can watch sponge divers in action and you'll often find pedaloes for hire. There are some water parks, and some operators provide safe activities for children.

Sailing. For sailors there are yachts (with or without crew) and *gulets* (elegant, traditional motor yachts) for hire. Holidays are available that combine a stay in a resort with a week's cruise.

Turkish Baths

No trip to Turkey would be complete without a visit to the *hamam*, or Turkish bath. There are three historic baths in Istanbul which cater specifically to tourists, namely the 16th-century Cemberlitas Hamamı, the 18th-century Çağaloğlu Hamamı (both in Sultanahmet), and the 16th-century Tarihi Galatasaray Hamamı in Beyoğlu. These places are worth a visit for their interior marble architecture alone, but the opportunity to experience a genuine Turkish bath should not be missed. There are usually separate entrances for men *(erkek)* and women *(kadın)*, but if there is only one chamber, then different times are set aside for men and women. Most are open from at least 8am to 8pm; longer hours for men.

Leave your valuables in a locker at the desk and get undressed in the changing room. Wearing a towel and bath-clogs, you will be shown to the steamy marble washroom, where buckets of hot water will be poured over you before an attendant sets to work with a coarse glove, removing dirt and dead skin and leaving you pink and glowing. You can also have a massage at this point (for an additional fee). Afterwards you retire to the changing room for tea or a drink, feeling completely relaxed and rejuvenated.

You can also try out mud and spa treatments, and massages, which are considered beneficial for many medical conditions.

Bird-watching

If you enjoy bird-watching, Istanbul and the Bosphorus is a special spot for migrating birds. Raptors are the main attraction, and most European species pass through, although some peak at different times. Look out for honey and common buzzards, the lesser spotted eagle and the Levant sparrowhawk.

Calendar of Events

January/February Camel-wrestling Festival in Selçuk.

March Festival of Victory, Çanakkale. Celebrates the Turks' successful defence of the Dardanelles against invading British warships in World War I. Includes performances by the traditional Ottoman army mehter band.

April Istanbul International Film Festival (<www.istfest.org>), lasting for two weeks, featuring new releases of Turkish and foreign films. Anzac Day, Çanakkale (25 April), a chance for Australians, New Zealanders and others to remember their dead on the Gallipoli Peninsula.

May Istanbul International Theatre Festival (<www.istfest.org>); Festival of Culture and Art at Selçuk and Ephesus, using the Great Theatre at Ephesus as a venue; Fatih Festivities, Istanbul, commemorating the conquest of Byzantium in 1453 by Sultan Fatih Mehmet (29 May).

June Istanbul International Music Festival, a world-class festival featuring big names in opera and ballet at venues including Topkapı Palace. Contact the Istanbul Foundation for Culture and Arts (<www.iksv.org>).

July Istanbul International Jazz Festival takes place at various locations around the city – contact the Istanbul Foundation for Culture and Arts. Istanbul Rock Republic Open-Air Festival, a 3-day event in Sayriyer.

August Assumption of the Virgin Mary, Ephesus. A mass conducted by the archbishop of İzmir at Mary's House (15 August).

End August–early September Rock 'n' Coke, Istanbul, Turkey's largest open-air rock festival.

October–November International Arts Biennale, Istanbul (odd-numbered years), major visual-arts event organised around an important political or philosophical theme – for further information contact the Istanbul Foundation for Culture and Arts (<www.iksv.org>).

Şeker Bayramı (30 September–2 October 2008; goes back 11 days each subsequent year) A three-day celebration marking the end of Ramazan. Presents and sweets are given to the children.

Kurban Bayramı (8–11 December 2008; goes back 11 days each subsequent year) Religious festival celebrating Abraham's willingness to sacrifice his son, with four days of feasting.

EATING OUT

Turkey has one of the world's richest cuisines, with influences derived from the many cultures of the former Ottoman Empire, and top-quality produce from Anatolia's lush farmland and fertile seas. Many dishes originated in the kitchens of the Ottoman sultans – in the time of Süleyman the Magnificent there were more than 150 recipes for aubergines alone. However, most tourists will be exposed to only a small range of Turkish dishes, unless they are invited into a Turkish home, or eat at one of the country's better restaurants. The majority of eating places in Istanbul and the Aegean resorts offer the standard fare of bread, salads, kebabs and seafood.

Kebab stand outside the Grand Bazaar

Meal Times

The typical Turkish breakfast, served between 7 and 10am, usually consists of fresh bread, butter and jam, with olives, cucumber, tomato, white cheese and perhaps a hard-boiled egg, washed down with sweet black tea. Try asking for *menemen*, a delicious dish of eggs scrambled with tomatoes, green peppers and onion.

In Turkey, people eat out regularly, and as a result

there are many restaurants, cafés and food stalls open all day and late into the evening. There are no set times for lunch and dinner, especially in tourist areas, and you can eat at almost any time of day.

A typical Turkish meal begins with a spread of *meze* (starters), washed down with *rakı*, followed by grilled meat, fish or kebabs, and rounded off with fresh fruit or milk puddings, and cups of the famous strong black Turkish coffee. Don't order a main course until you have finished the *meze*; you may be too full to appreciate it. It is perfectly acceptable to have a meal composed entirely of *meze*.

Where to Eat

Many of the eating places in Turkey specialise in serving a certain kind of dish. An average restaurant, offering a variety of typically Turkish food and drink, freshly prepared, is

A *büfe* is a street kiosk which sells snacks and soft drinks

called a *lokanta* or *restoran*, and may or may not be licensed. A *gazino* is a restaurant that serves alcohol, and usually also offers an evening floor show of belly-dancing and folk music. *Hazır yemek* ('ready food') means that you can choose your meal from heated trays of pre-cooked food.

A *kebapçı* specialises in grilled meats, notably kebabs served with *pide* and salad, while a *pideci* or *pide salonu* is a Turkish-style pizza parlour, dishing up tasty *pide* (unleavened bread) topped with minced lamb, eggs or cheese. You can enjoy lamb meatballs in a *köfteci*, tripe in an *işkembeci*, soup in a *çorbacı*, and milk puddings in a *muhallebici*. A *büfe* is a street kiosk which sells snacks and soft drinks. (See Recommended Restaurants, *pages 138–142*.)

WHAT TO EAT

Starters (meze)

Meze is the collective name given to a wide selection of appetisers, both hot and cold. They are usually presented on a tray at your table, or in a glass-fronted display case, and you can choose as few or as many dishes as you like. The more popular offerings include *kuru fasulye* (haricot beans in tomato sauce), *patlıcan kızartması* (aubergine fried in olive oil and garlic), *şakşuka* (aubergine, tomato and hot peppers in oil), *cacık* (yoghurt with cucumber and garlic), *biber dolması* (green peppers stuffed with rice, raisins and pine nuts), *sigara böreği* (cheese-filled pastry rolls) and a range of salads. *Çerkez tavuğu* (Circassian chicken) is a classic dish of chicken fillet cooked in a sauce flavoured with ground walnuts and paprika. *Meze* are served with fresh white bread to soak up the oil and juices.

Soups (çorba)

Turkish soups are usually thick and substantial. Try *düğün çorbası* ('wedding' soup, a mutton broth flavoured with

Fresh ingredients

lemon juice and cayenne, and thickened with egg), *mercimek çorbası* (red-lentil soup), or *işkembe çorbası* (tripe soup, believed to be a hangover cure). *İşkembecis* stay open until the early hours of the morning to serve bowls of tripe soup to peckish late-night revellers on their way home.

Main Courses

Ask anyone to name a typically Turkish dish and the likely answer you'll get is *kebap* – the well-known grilled, broiled or roasted meat. The most common varieties are *şiş kebap* (cubes of lamb threaded on a skewer and grilled over charcoal); *döner kebap* (literally 'revolving' kebab – a stack of marinated, sliced lamb and minced mutton roasted on a vertical spit, with slices cut off as the outer layers cook); *Adana kebap* (spicy minced beef moulded around a skewer and grilled); and *fırın kebap* (oven-roasted fillet of lamb marinated in yoghurt).

The ubiquitous *İskender kebap* is a dish of *döner kebap* served on a bed of diced *pide* bread with tomato sauce and yoghurt, topped with a sizzling splash of browned butter. *Çiftlik kebap* is a casserole of lamb, onion and peas. Meatballs of minced lamb, usually served with a tomato sauce, are called *köfte*. A classic Turkish dish, well worth asking for, is *mantarlı güveç*, a delicious stew of tender lamb, mushrooms, peppers, tomatoes and garlic baked in a clay dish and topped with cheese.

Seafood

The seas around Turkey abound with fish, and waterfront restaurants serve up the catch of the day, sold by weight. Fish is usually twice the price of meat, so not a cheap option. Choose your own fish from the display and find out how much it will cost before having it cooked. Some of the tastiest species are *levrek* (sea bass), *barbunya* (red mullet), *palamut* (bonito), *uskumru* (mackerel) and *lüfer* (bluefish). The best way to enjoy your fish is simply to have it grilled over charcoal; the waiter will remove the bones if you ask. Look out for *kılıç şiş*, chunks of juicy swordfish skewered with onion, pepper and tomato, and grilled.

Other kinds of seafood more commonly appear as *meze* – *kalamar* (squid), *ahtapod* (octopus), *karides* (prawns), *sardalya* (sardines) and *midye* (mussels). The mussels are either coated in flour and fried *(midye tava)*, or stuffed with rice, pine nuts, raisins and cinnamon *(midye dolması)*.

Desserts

Fresh fruit is often served to round off a meal – succulent *karpuz* (watermelon) and *kavun* (musk melon), *kiraz* (cherries), *kayısı* (apricot), *incir* (figs), *düt* (mulberries) and *erik* (sour plums) – but when it comes to prepared desserts, the Turks have a very sweet tooth. The most well known is *lokum* (Turkish Delight), a soft jelly, flavoured with rosewater and sprinkled with icing sugar. Another classic dessert is *baklava*, made of

Sweet names

Many confections have names which betray their origins in the harem – *dilber dudağı* ('lips of the beloved'), *hanım göbeği* ('lady's navel') and *bülbül yuvası* ('nightingale's nest').

Baklava selection

alternating layers of thin pastry and ground pistachios, almonds or walnuts, saturated with syrup. A traditional Turkish pudding shop *(muhallebici)* serves milk- and rice-based desserts like *fırın sütlaç* (baked rice pudding), *zerde* (a saffron-flavoured rice pudding), and *tavuk göğsü* (a combination of rice, milk, sugar and chicken breast). A more unusual dish is *aşure*, a sweet porridge made with cereals, nuts and fruit sprinkled with rose water, traditionally made from the 40 ingredients left in Mrs Noah's pantry as the flood waters receded and the Ark came to rest on Mount Ararat.

WHAT TO DRINK

The Turkish national drink is **çay** (tea). It is drunk throughout the day, in shops, cafés and offices, oiling the wheels of commerce, and sealing many a business deal. If you bargain for a carpet in the Grand Bazaar you will get through two or three glasses of *çay* before a price is agreed. Tea is usually served black, strong and sweet in small tulip-shaped glasses.

Turkish coffee *(kahve)* is strong, black and served complete with grounds in a small espresso cup, with a glass of water on the side. Sugar is added while brewing, so order *sade kahve* (no sugar), *orta kahve* (sweet) or *çok şekerli kahve* (very sweet). Leave it for a moment for the grounds to settle, and don't drain your cup. For instant coffee, ask for Nescafé.

Avoid drinking tap **water,** and stick to bottled mineral water, which is easily available everywhere – *maden suyu* is carbonated mineral water; *memba suyu* is still mineral water. A traditional Turkish thirst-quencher is *ayran*, a 50:50 mixture of yoghurt and mineral water, seasoned with a pinch of salt. Refreshing on its own, it's also often drunk with a meal. Fresh orange juice *(portakal sütu)* is available in season.

The national alcoholic drink is a very potent anise liquor called *rakı*. It is drunk as an aperitif, and indeed throughout the meal. It should be mixed half-and-half with iced water, with a glass of water on the side (when mixed with water it turns a pearly white, hence its nickname, *aslan sütü* – lion's milk).

Turkish **wines** *(şarap)* have a history going back as far as 7000BC, and some believe that European vine-stocks may well have originated here. Despite good quality local wines, the Turks are not great wine drinkers. Only a small proportion of the harvest goes into wine-making; they prefer beer and *rakı*. You can choose from a wide range of reds, whites, rosés and sparkling wines at very reasonable prices. Names to look out for include Villa Doluca, Çankaya, Kavak and Dikmen.

Tea seller in Sultanahmet

Turkish-made **beer** is also very good. The most popular (and cheapest) brand is Efes Pilsen, which is produced in Istanbul and sold in almost every bar and restaurant in the country. Imported labels are also common.

HANDY TRAVEL TIPS

An A–Z Summary of Practical Information

A

ACCOMMODATION (*oteller*; see also the list of RECOMMENDED HOTELS starting on page 130)

Turkey has a well-developed tourism industry, and accommodation is available to suit everyone. The Turkish Ministry of Tourism classifies hotels from one to five stars and a list is available from overseas tourism offices (see TOURIST INFORMATION).

Many hotels have their own web pages or are part of a booking group. Travel agents and tour operators provide information about hotels too, and they provide packages to suit. There are luxury city breaks and ones to suit lighter wallets. But even the luxury hotels offer tempting packages at quiet times. There are bargains to be had.

If you want a lively place in Istanbul, go to Taksim where many international hotels are located as well as some good inexpensive options. Peace and quiet is available in the Old City. Sultanahmet has plenty of reasonable establishments, as do Laleli and Aksaray.

The middle-range hotels provide rich pickings; many of them are very pleasant, the rooms equipped with TV, mini-bars etc. One-star hotels are not to be ignored: they are basic but comfortable. There are also *pensiyons*, often family-run and offering a very pleasant stay.

The Aegean resorts have very large numbers of hotels, self-catering villas and apartments, many of which are used by tour operators.

Resort hotels may be almost indistinguishable; the other end of the line is the historic 'special' hotel. These are usually in old houses, caravanserais or other ancient buildings and they usually offer 3 to 5 star amenities, but often can't have lifts because of the age of the building.

I'd like a single/double room.	**Tek/çift yataklı bir oda istiyorum.**
What's the rate per night?	**Bir gecelik oda ücreti ne kadar?**

AIRPORT *(havalimanı; havaalanı)*

The main airport is **Atatürk International Airport** *(Atatürk Hava-limanı*, tel: (0212) 663-6400, <www.ataturkairport.com>*)* near Yesil-köy, 24km (15 miles) southwest of the city centre. A free shuttle bus links the international *(dışhatları)* and domestic *(içhatları)* terminals.

The airport offers currency exchange, banks, a post office, car rental, a tourist information desk, restaurants and duty-free shops. A bus service called Havaş runs between the airport and the city centre, with services half-hourly between 6am and 11pm. Journey time is around 45 minutes, though the trip can take much longer during rush hour. Buses depart from the far side of the car park outside the arrivals hall and stop at Aksaray in the Old City, and Sişhane near Taksim Square. Taxis are faster and more convenient than the bus, taking only 20 to 30 minutes to the city centre. It's also possible to take the Metro (as far as Askaray) and onwards by tram (connect at Zeytinburnu) to the city centre *(see page 127)*.

Most low-cost airlines use **Sabiha Gokçen International**, Pendik, Asian Side (tel: (0216) 585-5000, <www.sgairport.com>). This has limited facilities, is 40km (25 miles) from Kadiköy and 50km (31 miles) from Taksim, and has no transport other than taxis.

Airports for the Aegean are at **İzmir** (Adnan Menderes Airport) and **Bodrum**. Some Aegean resorts are reached from **Dalaman**. Transfers to hotels and resorts are available from these airports.

B

BUDGETING FOR YOUR TRIP

In general, accommodation and meals cost less in Turkey than they do in Western Europe. Expect to pay from $70 (about £35) and up for decent accommodation in Istanbul, and $20 (£10) for a decent meal, including wine. The cost of public transport is minimal for buses, tram and ferries (around 1YTL/40p for a fixed-rate ride), and taxis are also inexpensive, at about 8YTL (£3) from Sultanhamet to Taksim. The most expensive individual sites are Aya Sofya and the Tokapı at £10–20. Mosques do not charge admission but welcome a donation.

CAR HIRE (*araba kiralama*; see also Driving)

A car is more of a liability than a luxury in traffic-packed Istanbul. However, if you plan to travel further afield, renting a car is a good way of getting around Turkey (especially since the rail system is not extensive). Car-hire rates vary considerably – local companies often charge substantially less than the big international chains, and it's possible to pay as little as £25 per day. You can get good rates by booking and paying for your car before you leave home, either directly through the UK office of an international hire company, or as part of a 'fly-drive' deal. Check that the quoted rate includes Collision Damage Waiver, unlimited mileage and VAT (KDV in Turkey). Note that hire-car insurance never covers you for broken windscreens and burst tyres. Unless you hire a four-wheel-drive, you will not be insured for driving on unsurfaced roads. You must be over 21 to rent, and you will need your passport, a valid driver's licence (EU model, with a photo) held for at least 12 months, and a major credit card.

CLIMATE

Istanbul enjoys a typically Mediterranean, temperate climate with warm, dry summers and cool, wet winters. July and August are the hottest months. The prevailing wind, the *poyraz*, blows down the Bosphorus from the northeast, and provides a welcome cooling breeze, but when the wind drops it can become uncomfortably humid, with occasional thunderstorms. The southwest wind, the *lodos*, usually brings storms on the Sea of Marmara. The best time to visit is in April, May and June when the days are pleasantly warm, and the shores of the Bosphorus are bright with spring flowers and blossoms. Winter is generally cold, wet and uncomfortable. Snow is not uncommon in the north in midwinter, though it rarely settles for more than a few days. The southern Aegean can have clear, sunny days, even in January.

Average daily maximum and minimum temperatures for Istanbul:

	J	F	M	A	M	J	J	A	S	O	N	D
°C max	8	9	11	16	21	25	28	28	24	20	15	11
°C min	3	2	3	7	12	16	18	19	16	13	9	5
°F max	46	47	51	60	69	77	82	82	76	68	59	51
°F min	37	36	38	45	53	60	65	66	61	55	48	41

CLOTHING

When it's hot, lightweight cotton clothes are the most comfortable choice, but evenings sometimes turn cool, especially in spring and autumn, so take along a jacket or sweater. Also take a long-sleeved shirt and sun hat to protect against the midday sun. In winter, warm clothes and a raincoat or umbrella will be needed.

Respectable clothing should be worn when visiting mosques and other Islamic monuments – long trousers or skirt, a long-sleeved shirt or blouse, and a headscarf for women.

COMPLAINTS (şikayet)

Complaints should first be made to the management of the hotel, restaurant or shop. If you're still not satisfied, then go to the tourist information office (see TOURIST INFORMATION). To avoid problems, always establish a price in advance. The tourist police are on Yerebatan Caddesi in Sultanahmet, tel: (0212) 528-5369/5150.

CRIME AND SAFETY (See also EMERGENCIES and POLICE)

You are far less likely to be a victim of crime in Turkey than you are in Western Europe and North America. Nevertheless, you should take the usual precautions against theft. Report any theft or loss to the police. If your passport is lost or stolen, inform your consulate. Drug use or trafficking is punished severely. Recent bomb attacks in Istanbul and resorts on the Aegean coast are of concern, but the chances of being involved are tiny, so don't let the risk spoil your holiday.

CUSTOMS AND ENTRY REQUIREMENTS

Visas. Visa regulations vary according to arrangements with different countries. Some nationals have to pay for a visa and others go free. UK, US and Irish citizens need a full passport, and require a 90-day visa that can be purchased from the visa desk before going through passport control in Turkey. At the time of going to press, the cost was £10, US$20 or €10 respectively, payable in cash.

Currency restrictions. There is no limit on the amount of foreign currency that may be brought in, but no more than US$5,000 worth of Turkish *lira* can be brought in or taken out of the country. However, remember that, due to inflation, the Turkish *lira* loses value rapidly and is hard to exchange outside the country.

The following duty-free items can be brought with you when you leave Turkey:

	Cigarettes		Cigars		Tobacco	Spirits		Wine
Canada	200	and	50	and	250*g*	1.1*l*	or	1*l*
UK & Ireland	200	or	50	or	250*g*	1*l*	and	2*l*
US	200	and	100	or	2kg	1*l*	or	1*l*

Antiquities. Buying and exporting antiquities is strictly forbidden. If you buy any object which might be classified as an antiquity (eg, antiques, old coins and even old carpets), make sure that it is from a reputable dealer, who can provide you with an invoice *(fatura)* stating its value and organise an export permit. 'Roman' coins and figurines sold by boys at archaeological sites are mostly worthless fakes.

D

DRIVING (See also CAR HIRE and EMERGENCIES)

If you bring your own vehicle, you will need a full driver's licence, an International Motor Insurance Certificate and 'Green Card' (make sure it's valid for the Asian sector if you plan to cross the Dardanelles or Bosphorus), and a Vehicle Registration Document. An official nationality plate must be displayed near the rear number plate, and headlamp beams must be adjusted if necessary for driving on the right. Motoring organisations have full details on requirements for Turkey and other countries that you may be driving through en route.

Wearing seat belts in both front and back seats is obligatory; on-the-spot fines can be issued for non-compliance. A red warning triangle and a fire extinguisher must be carried. Motorcycle riders and their passengers must wear crash helmets. Note that the minimum legal age for driving in Turkey is 18 years old, and that laws prohibiting drinking and driving are strictly enforced.

Rules of the road. Drive on the right, and pass on the left. Speed limits are 120km/h (75mph) on motorways, 90km/h (55mph) on highways and 40 or 50km/h (25 or 30mph) in towns and cities. Traffic joining a road from the right has priority, unless signs or markings indicate otherwise. There are fast, empty toll motorways between Istanbul, Edirne and Ankara and around İzmir

Fuel. In western Turkey there are plenty of petrol (gas) stations, and many are open 24 hours a day. However, there are as yet very few service stations on the toll motorways.

Parking. Watch out for signs saying *park yapilmaz* or *park yasaktır* (no parking) – the local police enforce parking regulations rigidly,

(international) driving permit	**(uluslararası) ehliyet**
car registration papers	**araba ruhsatı**
Green Card	**yeşil kartı**
Can I park here?	**Buraya park edebilir miyim?**
Are we on the right road for...?	**...için doğru yolda mıyız?**
Full tank, please.	**Dodurun, lütfen.**
I've broken down.	**Arabam arzalandı.**

and will tow away any illegally parked vehicles within a very short time. You will have to pay a fine to retrieve your car from the pound. The best bet is to look for an official car park *(otopark)*.

Traffic police. You can recognise the Turkish *Trafik Polisi* by their black-and-white baseball-style caps and two-tone Renault patrol cars. They patrol city streets and highways, and have the power to issue on-the-spot fines for traffic offences.

Breakdown. Most towns have a mechanic. Larger towns and cities have full repair shops and towing services. For rental cars there will usually be a 24-hour emergency telephone number, and the company will arrange for repairs or a replacement. For tyre repairs, look for a sign saying *lastikçi*, usually painted on an old tyre at the roadside.

Road signs. Main roads are well signposted; sights of interest to tourists are marked by special yellow signs with black lettering. Below are some common Turkish signs:

Çikis	exit	**Şehir merkezi**	city centre
Dıkkat	caution	**Tekyön**	one way
Dinlenme alani	rest area	**Yavas**	slow
Dur	stop	**Yolver**	give way
Gırılmez	no entry	**Yol yapimi**	roadworks
Park yapilmaz	no parking	**24 Saat Açık**	open 24 hrs

E

ELECTRICITY

Turkey operates on a 220-volt, 50-cycle current. An adaptor for Continental-style two-pin sockets will be needed; American 110-volt appliances will also require a transformer.

I need an adaptor/a battery.	**Bir adaptör/pil istiyorum.**

EMBASSIES AND CONSULATES *(elçilik; konsolosluk)*

Embassies are in the capital city of Ankara, but most countries maintain consulates in Istanbul:

British Consulate: Meşrutiyet Caddesi 34, Tepebaşı, Beyoğlu, Istanbul; tel: (0212) 334-6400

Canadian Consulate: Istiklal Caddesi 373/5, Beyoğlu, Istanbul; tel: (0212) 251-9838

Irish Consulate: Cumhuriyet Caddesi 26/A, Harbiye, Istanbul; tel: (0212) 246-6025

US Consulate: Kaplicalar Mevkii 2, Istinye, Istanbul; tel: (0212) 335-9000

EMERGENCIES

You will need a phonecard or credit card to call these numbers from a public telephone.

Police	**155**
Ambulance	**112**
Fire	**110**

ETIQUETTE

The Turks are by nature friendly, courteous and immensely hospitable – do not allow the persistent carpet-shop hustlers in places like Istanbul's Grand Bazaar to influence your opinion of them.

Most important of all is dress. You will notice that the people of Istanbul dress modestly, and avoid shorts and skimpy tops even in the heat of summer. When visiting mosques, wear long trousers or a skirt reaching below the knee, with a long-sleeved shirt or blouse; women should cover their heads with a scarf. At the Blue Mosque, scantily clad tourists are given robes to wear while visiting the mosque's interior. Mosques are open to tourists except during prayer times, especially on Fridays, the Muslim holy day. Remember to remove your shoes before entering a mosque or a Turkish house or flat.

You should never make jokes or insulting comments about Atatürk or the Turkish flag, or behave disrespectfully towards them (eg, don't climb on a statue of Atatürk to have your photo taken).

Body language can be confusing. If someone shakes their head, that means 'I don't understand'. 'No' is indicated by tilting your head back while raising your eyebrows, such as a Westerner might do to say, 'Pardon me? I didn't catch what you said'.

G

GUIDES AND TOURS

Official English-speaking guides can be hired through the local tourist office (see TOURIST INFORMATION) and through travel agencies and the better hotels. They are usually friendly and knowledgeable, and can prove invaluable if your time is limited. Freelance guides also hang around at the entrance to Topkapı Palace (make sure you agree on a price before hiring one). There are increasing numbers of tours offered for people with special interests: archaeology, Ottoman or Byzantine art and architecture, or tours of historic Jewish or Christian sites – the churches of Asia Minor or the footsteps of St Paul, for example. Excursions to places of interest are bookable from Istanbul and the Aegean resorts.

You can also book holidays which offer more than one focus, combining a city break in Istanbul with a resort holiday in the Aegean, or 14 days of cruising on a *gulet*. Alternatively, there are resort holidays where tourists remain within a complex and have little contact with Turkey at all.

We'd like an English-speaking guide.	**İngilizce bilen bir rehber istiyoruz.**
I need an English interpreter.	**İngilizce bilen bir çevirmene ihtiyacım var.**

H

HEALTH AND MEDICAL CARE

There is no free health care for visitors to Turkey. You should have an adequate insurance policy, preferably one that includes cover for an emergency flight home in the event of serious injury or illness. However, if you don't have insurance, Turkish hospitals are not prohibitively expensive, and they offer excellent treatment.

The main health hazards are the sun and the risk of diarrhoea, so use sun-block and a shady hat and be careful with food and drinks. Take a small pack of wet wipes, which come in handy for washing hands. For minor ailments, seek advice from the local pharmacy (*eczane*), usually open during normal shopping hours. After hours, at least one per town is open all night, called the *nöbet* or *nöbetci*; its location is posted in the window of all other pharmacies.

Vaccinations. There are no compulsory immunisation requirements for Turkey. Up-to-date vaccinations for tetanus, polio, typhoid and hepatitis A are recommended. A course of anti-malarial tablets is advised for anyone planning to visit the southeast in summer.

Where's the nearest pharmacy?	**En yakın eczane nerededir?**
Where can I find a doctor/	**Nereden bir doktor/**
a dentist?	**bir dişci bulabilirim?**
an ambulance/hospital	**bir ambülans/hastane**
sunburn	**güneş yanığı**
a fever/an upset stomach	**ateş/mide bozulması**

L

LANGUAGE

In the main tourist destinations many people are fluent in English, and many more speak a little. Locals will welcome any attempt you make to speak their language. The *Berlitz Turkish Phrase Book & Dictionary* covers most situations you are likely to encounter there. Below is the pronunciation of some Turkish letters:

c like **j** in **j**am
ç like **ch** in **ch**ip
ğ almost silent; lengthens the preceding vowel
h always clearly pronounced
ı like **i** in sir
j like **s** in plea**s**ure
ö approx. like **ur** in f**ur** (like German ö)
ş like **sh** in **sh**ell
ü approx. like **ew** in f**ew** (like German *ü*)

Numbers

0	sıfır	13	onüç	50	elli
1	bir	14	ondört	60	altmış
2	iki	15	onbeş	70	yetmiş
3	üç	16	onaltı	80	seksen
4	dört	17	onyedi	90	doksan
5	beş	18	onsekiz	100	yüz
6	altı	19	ondokuz	101	yüzbir
7	yedi	20	yirmi	126	yüzyirmi altı
8	sekiz	21	yirmibir	200	ikiyüz
9	dokuz	22	yirmiiki	300	üçyüz
10	on	23	yirmiüç	1,000	bin
11	onbir	30	otuz	2,500	ikibinbeşyüz
12	oniki	40	kırk	10,000	on bin

LAUNDRY *(çamaşır)*

Your hotel will be able to provide a laundry service, even if you are staying in a modest one-star establishment; usually, washing must be handed in before noon for return the following morning.

There are very few coin-operated launderettes. In Istanbul, try Active Laundry, Emin Paşa Sokak 14, off Divan Yolu, in the Sultanahmet district.

LOST PROPERTY (kayıp eşya; see also CRIME AND SAFETY)

Ask for advice from your hotel receptionist or the local Tourist Information Office *(see page 124)* before contacting the police.

I've lost my wallet/handbag/ passport.	**Cüzdanımı/el çantamı/ pasaportumu kaybettim.**

M

MEDIA

Television. The state-owned TRT *(Türkiye Radyo ve Televizyon)* broadcasts a number of nationwide TV channels. News in English is shown at 10.30pm on TRT-2, while international sporting events can be found on TRT-3. Many hotels have satellite TV with a huge range of viewing – BBC World, CNN, Sky, German, French, Italian and other European channels.

Radio. On shortwave radio you will get English BBC World Service and Voice of America. There are regular news summaries in English on TRT-3 (88.4, 94.0 and 99.0 MHz).

Newspapers. The English-language *Turkish Daily News* is published Monday to Saturday, and offers national and international news and features. You can buy British newspapers at several newsstands in Istanbul (in Sultanahmet, Laleli and Taksim) and in the main tourist resorts; they're usually a day late, and expensive. *Time*

Have you any English-language newspapers?	**Bir İngiliz gazeteniz var mı?**

Out do a weekly listings magazine with an English supplement. All the resorts have their own listings magazines and websites.

MONEY (See also CUSTOMS AND ENTRY REQUIREMENTS)

Currency. Turkey changed its currency in 2004, knocking off six noughts. The currency is the Yeni Turk Lira (YTL; new Turkish lira). At the time of writing, there were about YTL2.60 to UK£1. Coins *(kuruş)* are in 1, 5, 10, 20 and 1 YTL denominations. Notes are in 1, 5, 10, 20, 50 and 100 YTL units.

Banks and currency exchange *(banka; kambiyo; döviz)*. Banks are generally open 8.30am–noon and 1.30–5pm Monday to Friday. The most efficient banks are the Türk Ticaret Bankası, the Yapı ve Kredi and the AkBank. Rates of exchange and commission vary considerably, so it's worth shopping around. The rate in Turkey is always better than in the UK. In the more popular tourist resorts the banks have exchange booths which open independently of the main bank, often 8am–8pm including weekends. You can also change cash and traveller's cheques at the PTT office.

ATMs. A credit/debit card and an ATM is the fastest and easiest way to get cash in Turkey, and is cheaper than using traveller's cheques. ATM machines are commonplace in Istanbul and the resorts of the Aegean.

Traveller's cheques *(travelers çek)*. Generally accepted by middle- and upper-grade hotels, and by the banks mentioned above. The smaller branches may refuse to cash them.

I want to change some pounds/dollars.	**Sterlin/dolar bozdurmak istiyorum.**
Do you accept traveller's cheques?	**Seyahat çeki kabul eder misiniz?**
Can I pay with this credit card?	**Bu kredi kartımla ödeyebilir miyim?**

Credit cards *(kredi kartı)*. Major credit and debit cards are increasingly accepted in hotels, restaurants, tourist shops and car-hire companies. Some shops may ask you to pay a premium to cover the card company's commission.

O

OPENING TIMES

Banks: Mon–Fri 8.30am–noon and 1.30–5pm (some daily).

Currency exchange offices: daily 8am–8pm.

Museums: generally Tues–Sun 9.30am–5pm.

Post offices: main offices Mon–Sat 9am–5pm.

Shops: generally Mon–Sat 9.30am–7pm, closed noon or 1–2pm. Many tourist shops stay open later and on Sun. Grand Bazaar: Mon–Sat 8am–7pm.

Are you open tomorrow?   **Yarın açık mısınız?**

P

PHOTOGRAPHY *(fotoğrafçılık)*

Istanbul has plenty of instant photo shops where you can download and print the contents of your digital camera's memory card. Shops also stock a limited range of film; these days, buying a wider range of film is quite difficult.

The use of flash or tripod is forbidden in many museums, so always check before snapping away. Taking pictures of military subjects, such as airfields, and active archaeological excavations is forbidden. If you want to take photographs of the local people, avoid causing offence by asking permission first – some country people, especially women, may object.

POLICE (*Polis*; see also EMERGENCIES)

Turkey's civil police wear green uniforms. There is a police station (*karakol*) in every city and large town. In the countryside police duties are carried out by army personnel called the *Jandarma*; they have khaki military uniforms with a red armband. The *Trafik Polisi* patrol the highways, and man traffic checkpoints.

To telephone the police in an emergency dial **155**.

The tourist police in Istanbul have their headquarters at Yerebatan Caddesi, Sultanahmet, tel: (0212) 528-5369.

POST OFFICES (*postane*)

These handle mail, parcels and telephone calls, and often currency exchange as well; look for the sign 'PTT'. The counter marked '*pul*' sells stamps. Hours are Mon–Sat 9am–5pm for postal services, until midnight for phone calls.

The main post office in Istanbul is in Büyük Postane Caddesi (turn left, facing the ferries, at the Sirkeci tram stop); other branches are in the Grand Bazaar and at Galatasaray Square. Stamps can also be bought at tourist shops selling postcards. Postboxes are scarce – post your mail at your hotel desk, or at a PTT office. There are usually three slots – marked *şehiriçi* for local addresses, *yurtiçi* for destinations within Turkey, and *yurtdışı* for international mail.

A stamp for this letter/postcard, please.	**Bu mektup/kart için bir pul, lütfen.**
express (special delivery)	**ekspres**
airmail/	**uçak ile**
registered	**taahütlü**

PUBLIC HOLIDAYS *(milli bayramlar)*

There are two kinds of public holiday in Turkey – secular holidays, which occur on the same date each year, and religious holidays, which are calculated by the Islamic authorities according to the lunar calendar, and thus occur about 11 days earlier each year. Banks, post offices, government offices and many other businesses will be closed on the following secular holidays:

1 January	*Yılbaşı:* New Year's Day
23 April	*Ulusal Egemenlik ve Çocuk Bayramı:* National Sovereignty and Children's Day (anniversary of first meeting of Republican parliament in Ankara in 1920)
19 May	*Gençlik ve Spor Günü:* Youth and Sports Day (Atatürk's Birthday)
30 August	*Zafer Bayramı:* Victory Day (commemorates conquering of Greeks during the War of Independence in 1922)
29 October	*Cumhuriyet Bayramı:* Republic Day (anniversary of proclamation of the republic by Atatürk in 1923)

There are two national religious holidays (*Şeker Bayramı* and *Kurban Bayramı*), marked by three and four days off respectively. Seaside accommodation and public transport will be booked solid then, and ATMs may be low on cash. (See also CALENDAR OF EVENTS, page 98).

R

RELIGION

The national religion is Islam. Istanbul also supports Christian and Jewish minorities, and there are a number of synagogues and churches in the city. Details of local religious services can be obtained from the tourist office (see also TOURIST INFORMATION).

T

TELEPHONES *(telefon)*

Turkey is on the GSM mobile network (North American visitors will need a tri-band phone). You can make domestic and international phone calls from public phones at PTT offices, or phone boxes on the street. These accept either credit cards or telephone cards *(telekart)*, which can be bought at the PTT and at some newsstands and kiosks. There are also kiosks in post offices and private phone offices *(telefon ofisi)*.

For intercity calls (including calls to Üsküdar across the Bosphorus), dial 0, then the area code (212 in European Istanbul; 216 on the Asian side), then the number. To make an international call, dial 00 and wait for a second tone, then dial the country code (44 for the UK, 353 for Ireland, 1 for the US and Canada) and the full number including area code. Turkey's country code is 90.

TIME ZONES

Turkish time is GMT plus 2 hours in winter and GMT plus 3 hours in summer, making it 2 hours ahead of the UK for most of the year. Turkish clocks go forward on the last Sunday in March, and back on the last Sunday in September; from then until UK clocks go back on the last Sunday in October, Turkey is only 1 hour ahead of GMT. The table shows the time difference in various cities in **summer**:

New York	London	**Turkey**	Sydney	Los Angeles
5am	10am	**noon**	8pm	2am

What time is it?	**Saat kaç?**

TIPPING

In a restaurant it is normal to tip 10–15 percent, even if the bill says that service is included *(servis dahildir)*. Hotel porters who carry your bag to your room (this only happens in hotels of three stars and up) should get around $1 (50p). Taxi drivers don't usually expect a tip except on the airport route, though it is usual to round up the fare slightly. *Dolmuş* drivers never expect a tip. Gratuities of around 15–20 percent are looked for in barber shops and Turkish baths, and a few coins, worth around 10p, should be left for the attendant in public toilets, although many have a set fee.

TOILETS *(tuvalet)*

Public toilets are becoming smarter and more common. They can usually be found in museums and tourist attractions and near mosques. They are occasionally of the hole-in-the-floor variety, and sometimes lack toilet paper, so it is a good idea to always carry some with you. Actually, you are supposed to wash yourself and not put paper down the lavatory. It should go in a receptacle provided and most places have a notice asking users to put paper in the bin (because the plumbing can't cope). Some toilets are equipped with a special washing jet. *Kadınlar* or *Bayanlar* (Ladies) and *Erkekler* or *Baylar* (Gentlemen).

Where are the toilets?	**Tuvaletler nerede?**

TOURIST INFORMATION *(Turizm Danışma Bürosu)*

The Turkish Ministry of Tourism has branches throughout the country, but outside Istanbul and the main resorts they rarely have much information. The main offices are listed below:

Istanbul: Meydani, Sultanahmet (by the tram stop), tel: (0212) 518-1802/518-8754; Beyazıt Meydanı, tel: (0212) 522-4902; and in the lobby of the Hilton Hotel in Taksim, at the ferry station, railway station and airport.

İzmir: Akdeniz Mah., 1344 Sok. 2, Pasaport; tel: (0232) 483-6216 or 483-5117. Open daily 8.30am–7pm (to 5pm in winter).

Kuşadası: Liman Caddesi (on the corner opposite entrance to ferry and cruise ship terminal); tel: (0256) 614-1103. Open daily 8am–5.30pm in summer (to 8pm July and August); Mon–Fri 8am–noon, 1–5pm in winter.

Bodrum: Baris Meydanı (on quayside below St Peter's Castle); tel: (0252) 316-1091. Open summer daily 8.30am–7pm; winter Mon–Fri 8.30am–noon, 1–5.30pm.

The Ministry of Tourism overseas offices are:

UK: 170–173 Piccadilly, London W1V 9DD; tel: (020) 7355-4207; <www.gototurkey.co.uk>.

US: 821 UN Plaza, New York NY 10017; tel: (212) 687-2194/5/6; <www.tourismturkey.org>.

Where is the tourist office?   **Turizim bürosu nerede?**

TRANSPORT

Buses. Istanbul city buses, whether run by the city corporation (IETT) or private companies in accordance with city regulations, are cheap and frequent, but can be crowded, particularly at rush hour. Buy your flat-rate ticket from a kiosk before boarding. You can also purchase an **Abkil** electronic transit pass, a small stainless-steel button on a plastic holder with a computer chip inside, available from kiosks in Eminönü, Taksim Square and other nodal transport points. This is an almost hassle-free means of paying for your transport, particularly as it's also good for travel on trams, the Tünel, Metro and ferries. Simply place the Abkil against the little circular socket at the turnstile or front of the bus, and the fare will be deducted electronically. When most of its value is used up, have it recharged at an Abkil kiosk.

Dolmuş. A *dolmuş* is basically a shared taxi – a large saloon car or minibus that shuttles back and forth along a set route for a fixed fare. The departure and destination are shown on a sign in the windscreen. The driver waits at the departure point until all the seats are taken, then drops you off wherever you want along the way (*dolmuş* stops are marked by a sign with a 'D').

Ferries. The main point of departure for Istanbul's ferries is Eminönü, between Sirkeci railway station and Galata Bridge. The jetty nearest the bridge is marked *3 Boğaz Hattı* (Bosphorus Lines), for trips along the Bosphorus; next are the *2 Üsküdar* and *1 Kadıköy* jetties, for boats across to the Asian side; then comes the car ferry to Harem, near Haydarpaşa railway station, also on the Asian side; and finally, off to the right through a gate, is the Adalar (Princes' Islands) jetty. There are also ferries along the Golden Horn, which depart from jetties near the large Chamber of Commerce building just west of Galata Bridge. For all ferries, before departure buy a *jeton* from the ticket desk *(gişe)* where prices and timetables are displayed; or use your Abkil.

Sea bus catamaran. Sleek, modern passenger catamarans zoom around the city at rush hour, and out to the Princes' Islands several times daily. There are even Sea of Marmara routes to Yalova and Bandirma on the sea's southern shore for access to Bursa and the South.

Taxis. Istanbul taxis are bright yellow, and most are powered by clean-burning natural gas. They can be hailed in the street, picked up at a rank or ordered by telephone from your hotel. All taxis have meters and are required by law to use them. Most drivers are honest, but a few may try to rip you off by 'adjusting' the meter or doing conjuring tricks with your money. Fares increase by 50 percent between midnight and 6am. If you take a taxi across the Bosphorus Bridge, you will also have to pay the bridge toll. Few drivers speak English, so it's worth writing down your destination on a piece of paper.

Trains. There is a suburban rail service which runs from Sirkeci westwards along the coast to Yeşilköy near Atatürk International Airport. For the visitor it is only of use for getting to Yedikule and

Ataköy. Buy a flat-rate *banliyö* (suburban) ticket on the platform and keep it until the end of the journey.

Trams. Istanbul has a very useful tram service *(tramvay)* which runs along the European shore, through the Topkapı bus station at the city walls to Sultanahmet, Sirkeci (Eminönü), across the Galata Bridge and out past the Dolmabahçe Palace. The section of line between Eminönü and Yusufpaşa stops at Sultanahmet (Aya Sofya, Topkapı and the Blue Mosque), Çemberlitaş (Grand Bazaar) and Laleli (hotels). The tram is also very useful for getting to the airport, if you change onto the Metro at Zeytinburnu. You must buy a *jeton* from the ticket office and go through the turnstile; otherwise use your Abkil. Trams run every 5 minutes or so.

A restored 19th-century tram runs along İstiklal Caddesi from the top station of the Tünel to Taksim Square. Another runs from Usküdar down to Kadiköy on the Asian side.

Metro. Several lines of Istanbul's Metro system are in operation and two are particularly useful to visitors: starting in Aksaray Square, one goes northeast through the city walls to Istanbul's mammoth Otogar (intercity bus station), at which you can board a bus to any part of Turkey. Another line connects Atatürk Airport with Old Istanbul (see 'Trams' above).

Funiculars. Istanbul's tiny underground train, the Tünel, climbs the steep hill from Galata Bridge up to Pera. Trains leave every few minutes and take only 90 seconds to reach the top. A second funicular was added in 2006, linking Kabataş ferry port on the Bosphorus with Taksim Square.

Where's the nearest bus/ dolmuş stop?	En yakın otobüs/ dolmuş durağı nerededir?
I want a ticket to...	...'(a) bir bilet istiyorum.
Will you tell me when to get off?	Ne zaman inmem gerektiğini söyler misiniz?

TRAVELLERS WITH DISABILITIES

There are very few facilities for travellers with disabilities in Turkey. However, some of the more modern (and expensive) hotels do have wheelchair access. Check with your travel agent for information on hotels that offer facilities for travellers with disabilities. In Istanbul the pavements are rough and not made for wheelchairs or people with walking difficulties. Also, the extremely hilly nature of the place would make it very difficult for the disabled to move about.

TRAVELLING TO TURKEY

Scheduled flights from the UK. The national airline, THY (*Türk Hava Yolları* – Turkish Airlines; tel: UK central reservations: (0844) 800-6666, <www.thy.com>), flies to Istanbul three times daily from London Heathrow, daily from Stansted and five times weekly from Manchester. Cheap direct flights are also offered by British Airways (which also flies to İzmir) and easyJet.

Scheduled flights from the US and Canada. Turkish Airlines has regular non-stop flights from New York and Chicago to Istanbul. For details tel: 1-800 874-8875 (24hrs).

Most international airlines have regular flights to Istanbul.

Charter flights and package tours from the UK and Ireland. Available from Dublin, Gatwick, Manchester, Glasgow and a number of other British cities to İzmir, Bodrum and Dalaman (on the south coast near Marmaris) in summer. These are available as flight only or as part of a hotel or self-catering package holiday. Most tour operators also offer two-centre holidays, combining Istanbul with a coastal resort such as Kuşadası or Bodrum. There are no charter flights from North America to Turkey. Your best bet is to go via the UK or Europe.

By road. From the UK the main overland route to Turkey passes through Germany, Austria, Hungary, Romania and Bulgaria. The distance from London to Istanbul is approximately 3,000km (1,870 miles), for which you should allow at least four days of steady driving.

Driving time can be cut by heading to Italy and using the summer car-ferry services from Venice to İzmir or from Ancona or Brindisi to Çeşme. Reservations must be made well in advance.

By rail. Allow approximately three days for the full journey from London to Istanbul. The InterRail Global pass allows various periods of unlimited travel in 30 European countries, including Turkey. It is available to residents of the participating countries (for details tel: (08708) 371 371, <www.raileurope.co.uk>).

Sirkeci Station (Europe), tel: (0212) 527-0050
Haydarpaşa Station (Asia), tel: (0216) 348-8020

W

WATER

Tap water is safe, but may not agree with you, so you are advised to avoid drinking it. Bottled mineral water is obtainable everywhere. *Maden suyu* is carbonated mineral water; *memba suyu* is still mineral water.

WOMEN TRAVELLERS

Foreign women travelling in Turkey are occasionally subject to harassment from local men. A woman accompanied by a man is less likely to attract unwanted attention, but is not immune. The best strategy is to dress modestly, with long trousers, or a long skirt, and a long-sleeved, loose-fitting top. Walk with purpose. Don't meet their eyes. They will generally accept a firm 'no'. If not, raise your voice and a dozen knights in shining armour will rush to your aid. Treating women dishonourably is an offence to Islam and will not be tolerated by the locals.

Recommended Hotels

Finding accommodation in Istanbul is rarely a problem as the city has recently seen a boom in the hotel business. However, if you want a room in a particular hotel, it is best to book, especially during July and August. The main hotel areas are Laleli, Aksaray and Sultanahmet in the Old City, and around Taksim Square in the New City. Intense competition among the middle-range hotels means that you can often bargain for a lower rate, especially if you plan to stay for more than two nights. Many offer discounts for internet bookings; some offer discounts for cash.

As a basic guide we have used the symbols below to indicate prices for a double room with bath, including breakfast:

$$$$$	over £180 ($380)
$$$$	£100–180 ($210–380)
$$$	£70–100 ($150–210)
$$	£35–70 ($75–150)
$	below £35 ($75)

ISTANBUL

OLD CITY

Alzer $$ *At Meydanı 72, Sultanahmet, tel: (0212) 516-6262, fax: (0212) 516-0000, <www.alzerhotel.com>*. The Alzer is a comfortable hotel conveniently situated across from the Blue Mosque. Fresh cherries in your room. Noise from muezzin at dawn in front rooms. 22 rooms.

Ambassador Hotel $$$ *Divanyolu Ticarethane Sokak 19, Sultanahmet, tel: (0212) 512-0002, fax: (0212) 512-0005, <www. istanbulambassadorhotel.com>*. In the centre of Sultanahmet, close to the Blue Mosque and with views over the sea of Marmara, the Ambassador has nicely decorated rooms located in 19th-century restored townhouses. Grill restaurant and bar; breakfast on the top-floor terrace. 22 rooms, 2 suites.

Apricot Hotel $$ *Akbiyik Caddesi 75, Sultanahmet, tel/fax (0212) 638-1658, <www.apricothotel.com>*. An inexpensive hotel with a real family atmosphere. 24-hour hot water, air conditioning, cable TV and excellent breakfast. 18 rooms, two suites.

Armada Hotel $$/$$$ *Ahırkapı Sokak 24, Sultanahmet, tel: (0212) 455-4455, fax: (0212) 455-4499, <www.armadahotel.com.tr>*. Views of Aya Sofya and the Blue Mosque are a feature of this hotel, which has been erected as a reconstruction of a terrace of houses originally built for a 16th-century Ottoman Admiral. Two reputable restaurants and a bar; tango nights held on Sunday. 110 rooms.

Ayasofya Pensions $$$$ *Soğukçeşme Sokak, Sultanahmet, tel: (0212) 513-3660, fax: (0212) 513-3669, <www.ayasofyapensions. com>*. Between Aya Sofya and Topkapı Palace is a quiet, little cobbled street with beautifully restored wooden Ottoman houses. Rooms have en-suite, period furniture and Turkish carpets. Three restaurants (one in a Byzantine cistern), bars, a *hamam* and even a research library on old Istanbul. 63 rooms and seven suites.

Hotel Empress Zoe $$$$ *Akbiyik Caddesi, Adliye Sokak 10, Sultanhamet, tel: (0212) 518-2504/4360, fax: (0212) 518-5699, <www. emzoe.com>*. A small, intimate hotel near the Topkapı Palace. Each room is individually decorated and furnished and has its own bathroom of marble or terracotta. The garden incorporates the ruins of a 15th-century *hamam*. Pleasant roof terrace. 22 rooms, three suites.

Four Seasons Hotel $$$$$ *Tevkifhane Sokak 1, Sultanhamet, tel: (0212) 638-8200, fax: (0212) 638-8210, <www.fourseasons.com>*. Luxury hotel occupying a former prison, just steps from Topkapı, the Blue Mosque and Aya Sofya. Large, antiques- and *kilim*-filled rooms cluster around an open courtyard. Fine restaurant. 65 rooms.

Kariye $$$ *Kariye Camii Sokak 18, Edirnekapı, tel: (0212) 635-7997, fax: (0212) 521-6631, <www.kariyeotel.com>*. Beautifully restored, pastel-green wooden mansion in a peaceful location next door to the Kariye Museum. There is a pleasant garden restaurant (Asitane) specialising in Ottoman cuisine *(see page 138)*. 27 rooms.

Hotel Kybele $$$ *Yerebatan Caddesi 35, Sultanahmet, tel: (0212) 511-7766/7, fax: (0212) 513-4393, <www.kybelehotel.com>*. A small, intimate, family-run establishment with beautifully decorated rooms, antique furnishings and a delightful courtyard garden. The owner has a special liking for old lamps, which hang everywhere. 16 rooms.

Mavi Ev (Blue House) $$$$ *Dalbasti Sok 14, Sultanahmet, tel: (0212) 638-9010, fax: (0212) 638-9017, <www.bluehouse.com. tr>*. A friendly old hotel within touching distance of the Blue Mosque and Arasta Bazaar. The rooms are simply but attractively furnished, with a rooftop restaurant and a café/bar on the ground floor. 27 rooms.

Nena Hotel $$$ *Binbirdirek Mahallesi, Klodfarer Caddesi 8/10, Sultanahmet, tel: (0212) 516-5264-7, fax: (0212) 638-3059, <www. nenahotel.com>*. Boutique-style hotel just off the main road through Sultanahmet, with views of the Blue Mosque and Aya Sofya from the restaurant. Four deluxe rooms have private balconies. 29 rooms.

Hotel Nomade $$$ *Divanyolu Caddesi, Ticarethane Sokak 15, Sultanahmet, tel: (0212) 513-8172, fax: (0212) 513-2404, <www. hotelnomade.com>*. A delightful, reasonably-priced inn occupying a renovated old Turkish house, ideal for travellers. There is a rooftop terrace and the owners also run a bistro, the Rumeli Café, which is across the street. 16 rooms.

Sarniç Hotel $$$ *Kucuk Ayasofya Caddesi 26, Sultanahmet, tel: (0212) 518-2323, fax: (0212) 518-2414, <www.sarnichotel.com>*. In a restored townhouse with a rooftop terrace; simple, attractive décor, and a good restaurant. The hotel has the additional attraction of sitting right over a Byzantine cistern, which guests can visit. 16 rooms.

Yeşil Ev $$$$ *Kabasakal Caddesi 5, Sultanahmet, tel: (0212) 517-6785, fax: (0212) 517-6780, <www.istanbulyesilev.com/en>*. One of Istanbul's most famous hotels, set in a restored, four-storey wooden mansion behind the Blue Mosque, and once the home of an Ottoman Pasha. Rooms have Ottoman brass beds and period furniture. Beautiful garden restaurant. 19 rooms.

NEW CITY AND BOSPHORUS

Anemon Galata $$$ *Büyükdere Caddesi 11, Kuledibi Beyoğlu, tel: (0212) 293-2343, fax: (0212) 292-2340, <www.anemonhotels.com>.* One of a handful of 'special' hotels outside the Old City, this lavish boutique hotel beside the Galata Tower has it all, plush rooms, superb views from the rooftop bar/restaurant, and an ideal location.

Bosphorus Palace $$$$ *Yaliboyu Caddesi 64, Beylerbeyi (in Üsküdar on the Asian side), tel: (0216) 422-0003, fax: (0216) 422-0012, <www.bosphoruspalace.com>.* This hotel, occupying a former Ottoman residence (rebuilt after a fire in 1983), is one of the most exclusive of the city's 'special' hotels. Spectacular views. 14 rooms.

Büyük Londra $$ *Meşrutiyet Caddesi 117, Tepebaşı, tel: (0212) 245-0670, fax: (0212) 245-0671, <www.londrahotel.net>.* A fine old building (1892) uphill from the Pera Palas, and resonably priced. Built in the 'Orient Express' style, it mirrors the glamour of the age and much of the furniture dates from that era. 54 rooms.

Ceylan Inter-Continental $$$–$$$$ *Asker Ocagi Caddesi 1, Taksim, tel: (0212) 368-4444, fax: (0212) 368-4499, <www.interconti.com.tr>.* By Taksim Park, this hotel offers superb views over the Bosphorus and city. Specially adapted suites for the disabled. Restaurants provide Turkish, French and Californian cuisine. 390 rooms.

Çırağan Palace Hotel Kempinski $$$$$ *Çırağan Caddesi 84, Beşiktaş, tel: (0212) 258-3377, fax: (0212) 259-6687, <www.ciraganpalace.com>.* A prestigious, luxurious hotel in a restored 19th-century Ottoman palace that graces the shores of the Bosphorus. The hotel boasts two fine restaurants, and a health club, sauna, Turkish bath, shopping centre, plus indoor and outdoor pools. 324 rooms.

Conrad Istanbul $$$$$ *Yıldız Caddesi, Beşiktaş, tel: (0212) 227-3000, fax: (0212) 259-6667, <www.conradhotels.com>.* One of Istanbul's largest hotels, noted for its excellent food and comfortable rooms, furnished in contemporary Italian style and with extensive views. Pools, gardens, 3 restaurants, bars and a spa. 585 rooms.

Hyatt Regency $$$$$ *Taskisla Caddesi 1, Taksim, tel: (0212) 368-1234, fax: (0212) 368-1000, <www.istanbul.hyatt.com>*. This luxury hotel features the celebrated Harry's bar, where jazz is played, and also the Polo Lounge. Business centre, conference facilities and sports and leisure amenities including a Turkish bath. 380 rooms.

Pera Palas $$$$ *Meşrutiyet Caddesi 98-100, Tepebaşı, tel: (0212) 251-4560, fax: (0212) 251-4089*. The Orient Express hotel was built in 1892 and is still inhabited by the shades of Agatha Christie and Mata Hari. It is closed for renovation until late 2008 when guests will once again be able to enjoy the period atmosphere.

Ritz Carlton Istanbul $$$$$ *Suzer Plaza, Askerocagi Caddesi 15, Elmadag/Sisli, tel: (0212) 334-4444, fax: (0212) 334-4455, <www.ritzcarlton.com>*. Located in Dolmabahçe, the hotel towers above the Bosphorus. It offers everything – not just a *hamam*, but massage rooms for couples. Reservations required to dine or to take the elegant Bernardaud afternoon tea. 244 rooms.

Sumahan on the Water $$$$$ *Kuleli Cad 51, Çengelköy, Asian side, tel: (0216) 422-8000, fax: (0216) 422-8008, <www.sumahan.com>*. Already being hailed as one of the world's finest hotels, this converted *raki* factory on the shores of the Bosphorus is a true gem, with fabulously chic decor, one of the city's finest restaurants, Kordon, and heartstoppingly romantic views. A perfect hideaway from the bustle of the city. 18 rooms and suites.

Swissotel The Bosphorus $$$$ *Bayildim Cadessi 2, Macka Besiktas, tel: (0212) 326-1100, fax: (0212) 326-1122, <www.swissotel.com>*. One of the most pleasant of the modern international-style hotels near Taksim Square. Turkish bath, indoor and outdoor swimming pools. Six restaurants. 600 rooms, 17 suites.

Vardar Palace Hotel $$$ *Siraselviler Caddesi 54, Taksim, tel: (0212) 252-2888, fax: (0212) 252-1527, <www.vardarhotel.com>*. A central location, good for business, shopping and entertainment. The nicely restored hotel was built in 1901 and is a fine example of Levantine-Selçuk architecture. 40 rooms.

PRINCES' ISLANDS

Hotel Merit Halki Palace $$$ *Refah Sehitleri Caddesi 88, Heybeliada, tel: (0216) 351-0025, fax: (0216) 351-0032, <www.halkipalace hotel.com>*. A lovely 1850s Ottoman villa, converted into a hotel, with terraces and large gardens. Only 30 minutes from the city centre by boat, so ideal in summer. Swimming pool. 45 rooms and suites.

Splendid Palace $$ *23 Nusan Cadesi 71, Buyuk Ada, tel: (0216) 382-6950, fax: (0216) 382-6775, <www.splendidhotel.net>*. Founded in 1909, this Art Nouveau gem has been beautifully restored to offer guests a special retreat on the largest of the Princes' Islands. Beautiful, antiques-filled rooms; swimming pools; gardens. 70 rooms, four suites.

AIRPORT

Crowne Plaza Hotel $$$$ *Sahil Yolu, Ataköy, tel: (0212) 560-8100, fax: (0212) 560-8158, <www.ichotelsgroup.com>*. A luxury hotel overlooking Ataköy Marina , only 8km (5 miles) from the airport. Fitness centre, conference rooms, two pools. 170 rooms.

Radisson SAS Conference and Airport Hotel $$$$ *E-5 Karayolu, Sefaköy, tel: (0212) 425-7373, fax: (0212) 425-7363, <www.radissonsas.com>*. A newly renovated hotel with excellent conference, sports and health facilities. 245 rooms.

THE AEGEAN

If you plan a trip to the Aegean, the tour operators have many hotels and apartments available. For example, Kusadaşi has more than 300 hotels. The following are a few suggestions for the main centres:

BODRUM

Antique Theatre Hotel $$$$ *Kibris Sehitleri Caddesi 243, tel: (0252) 316-6053, fax: (0252) 316-0825, <www.antiquetheatrehotel. com>*. A luxury hotel and gourmet restaurant affiliated to the Chaîne des Rôtisseurs Association and, therefore, prestigious. 20 rooms.

Hotel Marina Vista $$$$ *Neyzen Tevfik Caddesi 226, tel: (0252) 313-0356, fax: (0252) 313-0361, <www.majestyresorts.com>.* A pleasant low-rise hotel, which is well situated at the quiet end of town near the marina. Recently renovated, the rooms are small-ish but comfortable, opening out onto a courtyard with a pool. 85 rooms.

Lavanta $$$$ *Yalikavak, tel: (0252) 385-2167, fax: (0252) 385-2290, <www.lavanta.com>.* Small, quiet hotel in a glorious location near Yalikavak village on the Bodrum Peninsula. Large pool, healthy eating with garden-grown vegetables and free-range eggs, bread oven and excellent wine cellar. Internet access. 8 rooms, 12 apartments.

Taskule $$$ *Plaj Caddesi 10, Yalıkavak, tel: (0252) 385-4935, fax: (0252) 385-2683, <www.taskule.com>.* On the water's edge, near shops, bars, restaurants and the harbour. There are 13 pretty rooms, each with sofa, fresh flowers and swanky bathroom, as well as a pool and bar.

ÇESME

Sheraton Çesme $$$$ *Sifme Caddesi 35, Ilıca, tel: (0232) 723-1240, fax: (0232) 723-1856, <www.sheratoncesme.com>.* Luxurious 5-star resort that has taken over from the Hilton as the best hotel in the area. Private beach, excellent food, rooftop bar, indoor and outdoor pools and spa.

IZMIR

Antik Han Hotel $ *Anafartalar Caddesi 600, Mezarlikbası, tel: (0232) 489-2750, fax: (0232) 483-5925, <www.otelantikhan.com>.* A historic 'special' hotel in the market area with simple rooms, bar, restaurant and courtyard garden. 24 rooms.

Kismet $$ *1377 Sok. 9, tel: (0232) 463-3850, fax: (0232) 421-4856, email: <kismetizmir@efes.net.tr>.* A couple of minutes' walk from the seafront, this is not atmospheric, but offers comfortable friendly, mid-range rooms and good food in a quiet side street.

Princess $$$$ *Balcova, tel: (0232) 238-5151, fax: (0232) 239-0939, <www.izmirprincess.com.tr>.* The Princess is on the outskirts of the city and is able to tap into the local thermal springs, so the health centre is a major attraction. 300 rooms.

KUSADASI

Atinç Otel $$ *Atatürk Bulvari 42, tel: (0256) 614-7608, fax: (0256) 614-4967, <www.hotelatinc.com>.* A modern, friendly 4-star hotel on the seafront in the town centre, with a bar, two restaurants (one a popular pizzeria) and a rooftop pool. 80 rooms and suites.

Club Kervansaray $$ *Atatürk Bulvari 1, tel: (0256) 614-2222, fax (0256) 614-2423.* Built in 1618, this is a restored caravansarai, complete with palm trees. The Turkish nights are highly recommended. Open March–November. 26 rooms, one suite.

Grand Blue Sky $$/$$$ *Kadinlar Denizi, tel: (0256) 612-7750, fax: (0256) 612-4225, <www.grandbluesky.com>.* A hotel facing the sea offering a full range of watersports, including diving, and its own stretch of private beach. Open April–November. 325 rooms and suites.

Kismet $$$ *Gazi Begendi Bulvari 1, tel: (0256) 618-1290, fax: (0256) 618-1295, <www.kismet.com.tr>.* One of Turkey's most enjoyable and famous hotels is stunningly situated on a seaside peninsula at the edge of town, surrounded by lush gardens. Guests have included Queen Elizabeth II and former US President, Jimmy Carter. The large rooms all have terraces and face either the harbour or the open sea. Private beach. 107 rooms.

SELÇUK

Kirkinca Konaklari $ *Sirince, tel: (0232) 898-3133, <www.kirkinca.com>.* This charming hotel with rooms and stand-alone houses all decorated with Turkish antiques is about 9km (5½ miles) from Selçuk, in the pretty, quiet village of Sirince. It makes a good base for exploring Selçuk, Ephesus and other sights in the region. Open all year, with central heating in winter. 5 rooms.

Recommended Restaurants

Istanbul offers a wide range of eating places, from kebab stalls to hotel-restaurants. The inexpensive *kebapcis* and *köftecis* in the back streets of Sultanahmet and Laleli often serve up far cheaper and tastier meals than the tourist traps. At the other end of the scale, you get what you pay for – exquisitely prepared Ottoman cuisine in the top hotel-restaurants, or the freshest of seafood in the many restaurants along the Bosphorus.

Below is a list of recommended restaurants. As a basic guide we have used the following symbols to give you some idea of what you can expect to pay for a three-course meal for two, excluding drinks:

$$$$	over £35 ($75)
$$$	£25–35 ($55–75)
$$	£15–25 ($32–55)
$	below £15 ($32)

ISTANBUL

OLD CITY

Asitane $$$ *Kariye Hotel, Kariye Sokak 18, Edirnekapı, tel: (0212) 534-8414.* Classic Ottoman cuisine and music in the setting of a peaceful garden neighbouring the Kariye Museum.

Hamdi Et Lokantasi $$ *Kalcin Sokak, Eminönü, tel: (0212) 528-0390.* Overlooking the Golden Horn, this unpretentious place specialises in grilled-meat dishes. Open for lunch only; no alcohol.

Havuzlu $ *Gani Çelebi Sokak 3, Kapalı Çarşı, tel: (0212) 527-3346.* Traditional Turkish cuisine in the heart of the Grand Bazaar. Open for lunch only. Closed Sunday.

Konyali $$$ *Topkapı Palace, tel: (0212) 513-9696.* Fine restaurant specialising in Ottoman cuisine, in a courtyard of Topkapı Palace with views over the Bosphorus. Open for lunch only; closed Tuesday.

Kumkapi $–$$$ A cluster of up to 50 seafood restaurants on the seafront below Sultanahmet, this is a wonderfully vibrant place to come and browse the menus, soak up the atmosphere and eat the freshest of fish. Take some change to tip the wandering musicians.

Pandeli's $$ *Mısr Çarşısı 51, Eminönü, tel: (0212) 527-3909*. Above the main entrance to the 500-year-old building of the Spice Bazaar, Pandeli's is famed for excellent Turkish-Ottoman food. Open for lunch only. Closed Sunday and public holidays.

Rami $$$ *Utangaç Sokak 6, Sultanahmet, tel: (0212) 638-5321*. The impressionist paintings of Rami Uluer, a Turkish artist, are displayed in this romantic restaurant set in a restored wooden mansion with period furniture. Serves seafood and Turkish dishes, and you can watch the sound-and-light show at the Blue Mosque from the terrace.

Seasons $$$$ *Tevkifhane Sokak 1, Sultanhamet, tel: (0212) 638-8200, <www.fourseasons.com>*. For a real splash-out foody meal, head for this rooftop restaurant at the Four Seasons Hotel, with magnificent views and world-class Asian-fusion haute cuisine.

Sultanahmet Meshur Halk Kofetcisi $ *Divan Yolu Caddesi 12, Sultanahmet, tel: (0212) 523-1438*. This bustling, family-run restaurant has been here since the early 20th century and is a Sultanahmet institution, popular with locals. The Koftecisi menu is simple – lamb kebab, meatballs *(kofte)* white bean salad and rice. No alcohol.

NEW CITY

Asir $$ *Kalyoncu Kulluk Caddesi 94/1, Beyoğlu, tel: (0212) 250-0557*. Situated about 500m off İstiklal Caddesi, the Asir has a relaxed atmosphere and a wonderful selection of *meze* (appetisers) and fish dishes; a popular spot for visitors and locals alike.

Café du Levant $–$$ *Ramhi M.Koc Museum, Haskoy Cadessi 27, Sutluce, tel: (0212) 250-8938*. Café in the grounds of Turkey's first industrial museum, serving French bistro food; wonderful views over the Golden Horn. Closed Monday.

Çatı $$ İstiklal Caddesi, Orhan A. Apaydın Sokak 20–7, Beyoğlu, tel: (0212) 251-0000. Pleasant rooftop restaurant serving Turkish and international dishes, including unusual Ottoman desserts such as candied tomato with walnut. Closed Sunday. Live Turkish band.

Changa $$$$ Siraselviler Caddesi 87/1, Taksim, tel: (0212) 249-1348. Situated in a striking Art Nouveau building, the Changa is Istanbul's premier fusion restaurant. The consultant chef is Peter Gordon, well known in London. Reservations strongly recommended.

Çiçek Pasajı $ İstiklal Caddesi, Galatasaray. The name means Flower Passage; not one restaurant, but several, grouped together along this 19th-century arcade. You can enjoy a full meal or just a snack of fried mussels and chips washed down with a beer.

Galata Kulesi $$$ Büyük Hendek Caddesi, Şişhane, tel: (0212) 293-8180. Enjoy the fine views from this restaurant set at the top of the Galata Tower. Turkish, French and international cuisine, with a belly-dancing show and live music in the evening.

Haci Salih Locantasi $ Anadolu Pasaji, İstiklal Caddesi 210, tel: (0212) 243-4528. A moderately-priced temple to Turkish home-cooking, with a cosy atmosphere and featuring lamb, vegetables and thick soups. No alcohol.

Kallavi 20 $$ İstiklal Caddesi, Kallavi Sokak 20, tel (0212) 251-1010. Small, upmarket and lively Turkish tavern with good food. Live traditional music at the weekend. Closed Sunday. No credit cards.

Leb-i-Derya $$$ Kumbaraci, Yokuşu 115/7, tel: (0212) 293-4989. With a fireside in winter, a terrace in summer and Bosphorus views year round, this glamorous restaurant is one of *the* places to be seen. The international menu ranges from a full English breakfast to a 40-spiced steak to chocolate fondue. All are heavenly.

Rejans $$$ Emir Navraz Sokak 17, Galatasaray, tel: (0212) 244-1610. Restaurant founded in the 1920s by White Russians. Menu includes classics such as borscht and beef stroganoff. Closed Sunday.

Vogue $$$ *Spor Caddesi, BJK Plaza, A Block, Floor 13, Süleyman Seba Caddesi, Beşiktaş, tel: (0212) 227-4404/2345*. Very chic restaurant offering contemporary American food and dishes from the Turkish tradition. Reservations essential.

BOSPHORUS

Beyti $$ *Ormon Sokak 8, Florya, tel: (0212) 663-2992*. An Istanbul institution famous for its grilled meats, most notably the skewered lamb fillets known as Beyti kebab. Weather permitting, meals are served in a charming garden. Near the airport; best reached from the city centre by taxi. Closed Monday.

Kanaat Lokantasi $$ *Selmani Pak Caddesi 25, Üsküdar, tel: (0216) 333-3791*. An institution and much admired, Kanaat was established in 1933 and is a family concern serving time-honoured recipes. It's a step away from the Üsküdar ferry terminal. No alcohol or credit cards.

Kız Kulesi $$$ *Salacak Sahil Yolu Kız Kulesi, Üsküdar, tel: (0212) 342-4747*. This is the restaurant in the Maiden's Tower. Diners are ferried across to the tower to enjoy traditional Ottoman/Mediterranean/Middle Eastern cuisine, as well as dancing and entertainment. Closed Monday.

Körfez $$$$ *Körfez Caddesi 78, Kanlıca, tel: (0216) 413-4314*. Fine seafood restaurant on the Asian side of the Bosphorus. If you call in advance the owner will have you ferried across on his boat. The speciality is *levrek tuzda* (sea bass baked in salt). No lunch on Monday.

Lacivert $$$ *Körfez Caddesi 57A, Kanlıca, tel: (0216) 413-4224*. On the Asian side of the Bosphorus, near the Sultan Mehmet Bridge, but with boat service from the European side, the Lacivert is famed for its Sunday brunch. DJs provide music to enhance the ambiance.

Memo's $ *Salhane Sokak 10/2, Ortaköy, tel: (0212) 260-8491*. A chic bar and restaurant that is always popular with young professionals, especially so in summer, when a waterside terrace is open. A disco on the premises begins hopping after midnight.

BODRUM

Kortan $$ *Cumhuriyet Caddesi 32, tel: (0252) 316-1300.* Seaside fish restaurant with an outdoor terrace. The menu is simple but the food is delicious. Great views of the sea and castle.

La Jolla Bistro $$–$$$ *Neyzin Tevfik Caddesi 174, Karada Marina Karşısı, tel: (0252) 313-7660.* Stuffed with drinkers in summer, out of season this is a charming wine bar and bistro on the seafront, with wonderful Mediterranean food and great margaritas.

CANAKKALE

Yalova $$$ *Gümrük Sok, Liman Caddesi, tel: (0286) 217-1045.* The best of a number of fish restaurants lining the seafront in Çanakkale. Good views, a rooftop terrace and convenient location near the ferry port. Open all year

IZMIR

Deniz $$$ *Atatürk Caddesi 174/1-A, Kordon, tel: (0232) 464-4499.* Commonly regarded as the best fish restaurant in town, with tables spilling onto the seafront pavement in summer. Open all year

KUSADASI

Ferah Balik Restaurant $$ *İskele Yanı Güvercin Parkı İçi, tel: (0256) 614-1281.* Laidback and slightly scruffy restaurant near the harbour, serving excellent seafood. Seafront terrace in fine weather.

SELÇUK

Kalenin Prensi (The Prince of the Castle) $$ *İsabey Mahallesi Eski İzmir Yolu 7, tel: (0232) 892-2087.* A jolly place with attractive gardens, a shady terrace and an ancient Roman menu alongside the standard Turkish fare. Open May to October only.

INDEX

Berlitz pocket guide

Istanbul & the
Aegean Coast

Third Edition 2008

Written by Neil Wilson
Revised by Beryl Dhanjal
Updated by Melissa Shales
Series Editor: Tony Halliday

Photography credits
akg-images 20, akg-images/Cameraphoto 17,
akg-images/Erich Lessing 18; Pete Bennett 6,
66, 71, 76, 78, 81, 82, 85, 88, 93, 96; Tony
Halliday 9, 10, 11, 15, 16, 22, 24, 26, 28/29, 30,
33, 34, 37, 38, 40, 43, 45, 47, 48, 49, 50, 51, 52,
56, 57, 58, 59, 61, 62, 63, 64, 65, 86, 89, 91, 95,
99, 100, 104, 105; Neil Wilson 55; Marcus
Wilson-Smith 13, 68, 75, 102; Phil Wood 42

Cover picture: Superstock

Printed in Singapore by Insight Print
Services (Pte) Ltd, 38 Joo Koon Road,
Singapore 628990. Tel: (65) 6865-1600.
Fax: (65) 6861-6438

Berlitz Trademark Reg. U.S. Patent Office
and other countries. Marca Registrada

Every effort has been made to provide
accurate information in this publication,
but changes are inevitable. The publisher
cannot be responsible for any resulting
loss, inconvenience or injury.

Contact us

At Berlitz we strive to keep our guides as
accurate and up to date as possible, but if you
find anything that has changed, or if you have
any suggestions on ways to improve this guide,
then we would be delighted to hear from you.

Berlitz Publishing, PO Box 7910,
London SE1 1WE, England.
fax: (44) 20 7403 0290
email: berlitz@apaguide.co.uk
www.berlitzpublishing.com